Ref

KT-194-724

n College

TY AND ISLINGTON
OLLEGE

FOR REFERENCE ONLY

Please do not remove from the Learning Centre

THE LEARNING CENTRE
The Marlborough Building
383 Holloway Road
London N7 0RN
tel: 020 7700 9283

M009258

VERY SHORT INTRODUCTIONS are for anyone wanting a stimulating and accessible way in to a new subject. They are written by experts, and have been published in 25 languages worldwide.

The series began in 1995, and now represents a wide variety of topics in history, philosophy, religion, science, and the humanities. Over the next few years it will grow to a library of around 200 volumes – a Very Short Introduction to everything from ancient Egypt and Indian philosophy to conceptual art and cosmology.

Very Short Introductions available now:

Available soon:

M009258

For more information visit our web site

www.oup.co.uk/vsi

Kevin Passmore

FASCISM

A Very Short Introduction

OXFORD
UNIVERSITY PRESS

OXFORD

UNIVERSITY PRESS

Great Clarendon Street, Oxford OX2 6DP

Oxford University Press is a department of the University of Oxford.
It furthers the University's objective of excellence in research, scholarship,
and education by publishing worldwide in

Oxford New York

Auckland Bangkok Buenos Aires Cape Town Chennai
Dar es Salaam Delhi Hong Kong Istanbul Karachi Kolkata
Kuala Lumpur Madrid Melbourne Mexico City Mumbai Nairobi
São Paulo Shanghai Singapore Taipei Tokyo Toronto

with an associated company in Berlin

Oxford is a registered trade mark of Oxford University Press
in the UK and in certain other countries

Published in the United States
by Oxford University Press Inc., New York

© Kevin Passmore 2002

The moral rights of the author have been asserted
Database right Oxford University Press (maker)

First published as a Very Short Introduction 2002

All rights reserved. No part of this publication may be reproduced,
stored in a retrieval system, or transmitted, in any form or by any means,
without the prior permission in writing of Oxford University Press,
or as expressly permitted by law, or under terms agreed with the appropriate
reprographics rights organizations. Enquiries concerning reproduction
outside the scope of the above should be sent to the Rights Department,
Oxford University Press, at the address above

You must not circulate this book in any other binding or cover
and you must impose this same condition on any acquirer

British Library Cataloguing in Publication Data

Data available

Library of Congress Cataloging in Publication Data

Data available

ISBN 0-19-280155-4

1 3 5 7 9 10 8 6 4 2

Typeset by RefineCatch Ltd, Bungay, Suffolk
Printed in Spain by Book Print S. L., Barcelona

C.I.C.
MARLBOROUGH BLDG.
383 HOLLOWAY ROAD
LONDON N7 0RN

Fascism has an enigmatic countenance because in it appears the most counterpoised contents. It asserts authoritarianism and organises rebellion. It fights against contemporary democracy and, on the other hand, does not believe in the restoration of any past rule. It seems to pose itself as the forge of a strong State, and uses means most conducive to its dissolution, as if it were a destructive faction or a secret society. Whichever way we approach fascism we find that it is simultaneously one thing and the contrary, it is A and not A . . .

José Ortega y Gasset, 'Sobre el Fascismo' (1927)

Contents

Acknowledgements

Inevitably, this book synthesizes an enormous range of existing scholarship, and it is impossible to express fully my debt to all the scholars upon whose work I have drawn. I have benefited particularly from reading the works of Martin Blinkhorn, Michael Burleigh and Wolfgang Wipperman, Roger Eatwell, Roger Griffin, Stanley Payne, and Dave Renton. Mark Donovan, Martin Durham, and Maura Hametz helped me with particular parts of the book. Mark Donovan, along with Stefan Berger, Pat Hudson, and Garthine Walker, read all or part of the manuscript. I would also like to express my gratitude to the anonymous readers for their helpful suggestions and to Katharine Reeve for her encouraging and sympathetic editorship.

List of illustrations

List of maps

Chapter 1

Scenes from the history of fascism

Aigues-Mortes, France, 1893

In the late 19th century, the saltworks of Mediterranean France
were largely unmechanized, and the task of lifting salt was an
exceptionally exhausting form of labour. Under the blazing August
sun, workers pushed heavy barrowloads of salt along wooden
planks to the top of an ever-higher heap of salt. Since the work was
seasonal, poor, itinerant workers inevitably performed it, and
because France suffered from a shortage of labour, many of these
were immigrant Italians.

On 16 August 1893, at the saltworks of Aigues-Mortes, unfounded
rumours that Italians had killed three French workers triggered a
veritable manhunt against the unlucky migrants. The next morning,
the police escorted as many Italians as possible to the railway
station. On the way the frightened workers were savagely assaulted
by Frenchmen. At least six Italians were killed en route, and two
elsewhere. Eventually, the Italians were given refuge in the
medieval Tour de Constance at Aigues-Mortes. No one can say how
many more Italians met anonymous deaths in the saltmarshes in
the following two days.

Brawls between French and immigrant workers were common
during this period, though not usually mortal. Antipathy to foreign

workers marked all political tendencies – at Aigues-Mortes one column of French workers was headed by a red flag. Yet there was something novel about the Aigues-Mortes massacre.

By coincidence, Maurice Barrès, a writer seen by some as one of the inventors of fascism, had set his 1890 novel, *Le Jardin de Bérénice*, in Aigues-Mortes, and had used the Tour de Constance as the symbol of a new kind of nationalism. Barrès rejected the liberal and democratic view that the nation was the expression of the rational interests of individual (male) inhabitants of France. For him, the nation emanated from a spiritual feeling beyond normal human understanding – a view shaped by then trendy psychological ideas about the collective human unconscious, and by the literary symbolist movement, which believed that art could access the hidden myths underlying human behaviour. Barrès saw the nation as the product of history, tradition, and of the long contact of the French peasantry with the national soil. From the top of the Tour de Constance the hero of *Le Jardin de Bérénice* is able to see the vastness of the French countryside. He communicates with France's medieval past, and realizes that he, as an individual, 'is just a single minute in this vast country'. Barrès's hero was at one with the French soil. An immigrant never could be.

Barrès might seem to be just another self-obsessed artist, convinced that he possessed the keys to the human soul. There is indeed plenty of that kind of arrogance in Barrès's writings. Yet there was more to him than this. In 1889 Barrès had been elected to represent the eastern city of Nancy in parliament as a follower of General Boulanger, a soldier who had promised to cleanse France of corrupt parliamentary politicians. Barrès's electoral campaign, moreover, had exploited the antisemitism of the Nancy population. Increasingly, he saw nationalism as the solution to all problems. A few weeks before the Aigues-Mortes massacre, Barrès wrote a series of pieces for the daily *Le Figaro*, under a headline that needs little elucidation: 'Against foreigners'. These articles were published at a time of poor relations between Italy and France, when Italian immigrants were regarded as potential spies. Barrès was not directly responsible for the events at Aigues-Mortes, but his novels and political journalism linked popular xenophobia with the intellectual origins of fascism. In 1898 Barrès referred to himself as a 'national socialist'.

Rome, 16 November 1922

Newly appointed prime minister, Benito Mussolini presented his administration to parliament on 16 November 1922. Although there were only 32 Fascists in the chamber, Mussolini was supremely confident. Journalists found him in expansive mood, posing as a man of will and decision. He obviously delighted in the luxury hotel in which he had taken up residence (with his shabbily dressed armed guard).

It was unclear what Fascism would mean in practice. The Blackshirts had not staged the 'March on Rome' to see Mussolini become another high-living prime minister in the Liberal regime. They expected a thoroughgoing 'national revolution'. Yet Mussolini did not owe his elevation to the Blackshirts alone, for ruling liberal politicians had offered Mussolini the premiership well before the Blackshirts arrived in the capital. Who would have the upper hand – the Blackshirts or Mussolini's conservative allies?

Then there was Mussolini himself. He told a *Times* journalist that he intended to improve living standards for the poor, and that the bourgeoisie had some nasty surprises in store. Others learned that he would proclaim himself 'the prince of reactionaries' and create a special ministry of police, or that he intended to bend the people to his will in a new national community. Mussolini was hardly less contemptuous of his own lieutenants than he was of established politicians.

Mussolini's speech in parliament clarified little. He multiplied assurances to the establishment, claiming that constitutional government was safe. Yet he threatened deputies with Fascist revolutionaries if they refused to grant him special legislative powers.

Turnu Severin, Romania, May 1924

Despite the weight of evidence against him, Corneliu Codreanu, a 24-year-old law student at Iaşi University, wasn't especially worried as he awaited the verdict in his trial for murder – perhaps because the jurors all wore swastika badges in their lapels. Even the prosecuting lawyer had spoken of extenuating circumstances: 'Anarchy had penetrated the university because of the large number of foreigners', he said, adding an appeal for 'Romania for the Romanians'.

Romania was rewarded for its part in the Allied victory in the Great War with lands carved from the Austro-Hungarian and Russian empires. These 'new territories' included substantial minorities of Jews, Hungarians, and Germans, who were especially numerous amongst the urban business and professional classes. Romanians agreed that the 'new territories' must be fused into a homogeneous Romanian national state, and that ethnic Romanians should replace Jews in business and the professions. Some minorities would be 'assimilated'; others – especially Jews – would be excluded.

Ethnic Romanian students like Codreanu at the Iaşi campus in Moldavia were at the forefront of the struggle to 'Romanianize' the new territories – intellectuals in Romania had traditionally seen themselves as the nationalist vanguard. These radical nationalists, Romania's future lawyers and doctors, held Jews responsible for the brief upsurge of left-wing activity that had followed the Great War. Codreanu felt that Romanian students were 'smothered by the immense mass of Jewish students from Bessarabia, all agents of communist propaganda'. In 1922 a campaign for the restriction of Jewish enrolment in universities (a

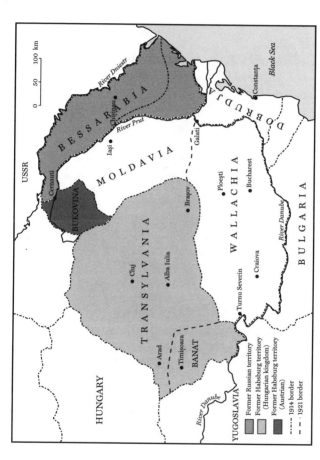

Map 1. Romania

Scale: 0 50 100 km

USSR

River Dniestr

BESSARABIA

Cernăuţi

Chişinău

River Prut

Iaşi

BUKOVINA

MOLDAVIA

Galaţi

DOBRUDJA

Constanţa

Black Sea

HUNGARY

Arad

Cluj

Alba Iulia

TRANSYLVANIA

Braşov

Ploeşti

WALLACHIA

Bucharest

Timişoara

BANAT

Turnu Severin

Craiova

River Danube

YUGOSLAVIA

River Danube

BULGARIA

Former Russian territory

Former Habsburg territory (Hungarian kingdom)

Former Habsburg territory (Austrian)

----- 1914 border

– – – 1921 border

1. Codreanu inspects his Legionnaires. Note the peasant costume underneath his city overcoat and hat.

numerus clausus) erupted across Romania. Radical nationalists saw the government's rejection of the restriction as evidence of the authorities' partiality to Romania's enemies. Yet a student charged with assassinating an alleged police informer was acquitted by the courts.

In October 1924 Codreanu murdered the Iaşi prefect of police, an opponent of the student movement. A first attempt at trying Codreanu in the Moldavian town of Focşiani was abandoned because of antisemitic riots. In May the trial reconvened in the small town of Turnu Severin on the distant Danube, which the government hoped would be quieter. Yet thousands of Codreanu supporters stirred up antisemitic feeling. The whole town wore national colours, and many sported swastikas. The Romanian Bar Association tried to ensure that none of its members represented the prefect's widow. Although the prosecution did manage to secure the services of a weak counsel, Codreanu was acquitted, to no one's surprise.

Codreanu is best known to history as the leader of the Legion of the Archangel Michael, otherwise known as the Iron Guard. This fascist organization fought a bitter battle, punctuated by political murders, against a succession of constitutional governments, and then against a royal dictatorship. In November 1938 the royal government suppressed the Iron Guard, and garrotted Codreanu.

The Kroll Opera House, Germany, 23 March 1933

The opening session of the last Reichstag took place in the Kroll Opera House, situated on the Tiergarten in central Berlin, for the Reichstag building had been destroyed by fire a few weeks previously. Inside the hall a huge swastika flag hung behind the platform occupied by the cabinet and president of the Reichstag. To get to the hall, deputies had to run the gauntlet of insolent swastika-wearing youths massed on the wide square in front, who called them 'Centrist pigs' or 'Marxist sows'. Communist deputies had been imprisoned because of the Party's alleged involvement in burning down the Reichstag building. A few socialists were also incarcerated, and another was arrested on entering the building. Nazi stormtroopers lined up behind the socialists and blocked the exits.

Only one item lay before the Reichstag: an Enabling Law, giving the chancellor the power to issue laws without the approval of the Reichstag, even where they deviated from the constitution. Since the law entailed a change to the constitution, a two-thirds majority was required, and the Nazis therefore needed conservative support. Hitler's speech introducing the proposed law reassured conservatives that neither the existence of parliament nor the position of their icon, President Hindenburg, were threatened. It was understood that conservatives would vote for the Enabling Act.

Frowning intensely, Hitler read his declaration with an unusual self-possession. Only in calling for public execution of the author of the Reichstag fire, and in uttering dark threats against the socialists, did his more habitual frenzy surface. At the end of his speech Nazi deputies thundered out 'Deutschland über alles'.

In reply, the socialist Otto Wels courageously invoked the 'principles of humanity and justice, of freedom and socialism'. Yet the French ambassador remembered that he spoke with the air of a beaten child. His voice choking with emotion, Wels concluded by expressing best wishes to those already filling concentration camps and prisons. Hitler, who'd been feverishly taking notes, passionately responded by accusing socialists of having persecuted the Nazis for 14 years. In fact, Nazis had been punished only mildly, if at all, for their illegal activities. Socialists heckled, but stormtroopers behind them hissed 'you'll be strung up today'.

The Enabling Law was passed by 444 votes against the 94 of the socialists. It destroyed the rule of law and laid the basis for a new kind of authority based, in principle, on the will of the Führer. In practice it licensed the Nazis to act as they saw fit, in the 'higher interests of the German people', against anyone deemed to be an enemy of the Reich. The socialists were the next victims.

Chapter 2
'A and not A': what is fascism?

The term 'fascist' was first applied to a political movement combining ultranationalism with hostility both to the left and to established conservatism by Mussolini in 1919. Three years later Mussolini came to power at the head of a coalition backed by conservatives, and in 1926 he began to establish a full-scale dictatorship. By this time Fascism was widely admired by a plethora of distinguished political and literary figures outside Italy, not all of them on the right. During the economic, social, and political crisis beginning in 1929 Nazism made its breakthrough and came to power in January 1933. While Mussolini set out to create a 'totalitarian' society, Hitler embarked on the creation of a racial Utopia, a dream that entailed the elimination of Jews from Germany and military conquest of Eastern Europe. Meanwhile, significant fascist movements emerged in many other European countries and in Brazil.

Increasingly, the struggle between fascism and its opponents dominated the political landscape. Popular Fronts against fascism won power in France and Spain. Even in countries where there was little indigenous fascism, such as Sweden, left-wing governments presented innovative welfare and agricultural price support policies as means to fend off a potential fascist threat. Mussolini's and Hitler's military expansionism spread the conflict between fascism and antifascism to international relations too, forcing even the pariah Soviet Union out of its diplomatic isolation. From 1939 the Nazis' conquest of much of Europe permitted fascists briefly to enter government in countries where they would otherwise have remained in opposition, notably Croatia and Romania. But the insatiable desire of Fascists and Nazis for conquest created an international coalition which eventually crushed fascism at the cost of millions of people dead, wounded, and displaced.

After 1945 fascism's legacy continued to structure the political landscape. Political leaders in the Allied countries drew legitimacy from their role in defeating fascism, while governments in Italy and Germany claimed descent from the antifascist resistance. The left accused conservative anticommunists of being fascists, while the right equated communism with fascism. Given that fascism has become an all-purpose term of abuse, it is no surprise that those who mimic fascism have not hitherto become politically relevant, but movements that owe something to fascism, especially its nationalism and racism, made something of a breakthrough during the late 1990s.

Along with liberalism, conservatism, communism, socialism, and democracy, fascism is one of the great political ideologies that shaped the 20th century. In the 21st century interest in the history of fascism and its crimes is perhaps greater than ever. Yet how can we make sense of an ideology that appeals to skinheads and intellectuals; denounces the bourgeoisie while forming alliances with conservatives; adopts a macho style yet attracts many women; calls for a return to tradition and is fascinated by technology; idealizes the people and is contemptuous of mass society; and preaches violence in the name of order? Fascism, as Ortega y Gasset says, is always 'A and not A'.

There is another even more fundamental problem. The diversity of movements and regimes under consideration is arguably so great that to give them all the label 'fascist' would obscure what is distinctive about each of them. Does use of the term 'fascist' deny the uniquely evil nature of Nazism? Is it better to classify Nazism and Stalinism together as examples of totalitarianism? The very title of this book implies that I think there *is* something to be gained by using the concept of fascism. So I must begin by justifying this contention.

Those who study the literature on fascism in the hope of pinning down a precise meaning often throw up their hands in despair – 'it all depends on definition', they sigh wearily, 'so it must be a matter of personal opinion'. Yes, everything does depend on definition, but this should not be a reason for abandoning the concept. At the risk of straining the patience of the reader, I want to explain what we require from definitions – how do we define definitions?

One justification for using the term fascism (or any other such concept) is that it enables appreciation and comparison of tendencies common to more than one country and period. The recognition of such generalities is not incompatible with the uniqueness of particular movements and regimes. Indeed, only through comparison can we discover what is unique about a particular case. Sometimes unique features – such as the Nazis' drive to create a 'racial state' – are very important. All the same, it is quite legitimate to emphasize either general or specific aspects, according to one's interests and questions – so long as the concepts used allow for other perspectives.

It does not follow that all approaches are equally useful. A concept must be framed in such a way that it can be subjected to criticism and possible contradiction. For example, the concept of race as it is deployed by fascists is no more than a prejudice or article of faith, which is not subject to critical analysis. Behind racism is a sort of double-think that renders belief in the determining importance of race immune to contrary evidence. Thus, if one is convinced that

Jews are responsible for the evils of capitalism, or that Asians are bad drivers (a common prejudice in the contemporary racist), one can endlessly pile up examples of Jewish capitalists and bad Asian drivers, for 'they' are 'all the same'. But evidence of the misdeeds of non-Jewish capitalists or poor driving by whites is not treated in the same way. If it is noticed at all, it will be dismissed as an individual aberration, and not attributed to ethnic origin – one will not say 'typical of them' when a white driver pulls out of a road without looking for oncoming traffic. In effect, 'their' behaviour is determined by their race, while 'we' are individuals. Since it rests on unfalsifiable assumptions of this ilk, Hitler's explanation of the emergence of Nazism as the result of a struggle of Aryan and Jewish races can be rejected completely as a means of understanding fascism. Our definitions must permit critical analysis and investigation.

Scholarly definitions are not so easy to dispose of as those of fascists themselves. Most have *some* value. So how do we say which definitions are preferable? Besides being potentially falsifiable, definitions must also illuminate and make sense of the things that we know about the world – we couldn't even recognize fellow human beings if we didn't have a concept of a person. The diversity of human life is such that no concept can account for *every* feature of any object of study, and the study of fascism doesn't depart from this rule. But some concepts explain *more* than others, so we must ask how much of our object of study, and which aspects of it, are explained by a particular concept.

Difficulties arise when scholars claim that their pet theory provides the *only* way to understand fascism. Since any given political movement is too complex to be encompassed within a single concept, they soon encounter evidence that won't 'fit'. They get around the problem by claiming that their theory explains the most *important* aspects of fascism. Difficult features are dismissed as less significant. Unfortunately, this division of the features of fascism into primary and secondary is arbitrary – or determined by political preference.

I want now to review in a little more detail some of the principal ways in which fascism has been understood. Since there are so many theories of fascism it is necessary to simplify somewhat. I have therefore chosen to group theories according to whether they see the conservative or the radical sides of fascism as fundamental. Whilst each is useful, none represents the only way of understanding fascism. At the end of the chapter I shall propose a definition, which I feel is more complete in the sense described above. It incorporates the strong points of other theories, and is able to deal with the contradictions of fascism highlighted in the previous chapter. Even this definition cannot encompass all aspects of individual cases, but it may assist in our understanding of the phenomenon.

Marxist approaches

In its simplest form, Marxism assumes that modern society is divided into two fundamental classes: the bourgeoisie, or capitalists, who own the means of production (tools, factories) but do not engage in manual labour; and the working classes, or proletariat, who engage in manual labour but do not own the means of production. Capitalists and proletarians struggle for ownership of the means of production and control over the state. Between these two great classes are the petty bourgeoisie, including self-employed traders, small businessmen, peasants, and white-collar workers. The petty bourgeoisie is uncertain whether to side with capital or labour; it owns property and yet is exploited by big business.

Marxist approaches to fascism all emphasize its links with capitalism. The most influential early definition was that of the Communist International in 1935, which stated that 'Fascism in power is the open, terroristic dictatorship of the most reactionary, the most chauvinistic, the most imperialistic elements of finance capitalism'. It was held that when pressure from the proletariat for the destruction of capitalism rose to extreme proportions, capitalists resorted to terror to defend their control over the means of production. For the Communist International, the current crisis of capitalism was so serious that a conventional dictatorship was inadequate. Therefore capitalists used the mass fascist movement to destroy socialism. According to the 1935 definition, fascism was not a *creation* of the capitalists, for it recruited from the petty bourgeoisie, which had real grievances against big capital. Nevertheless, capitalists were able to persuade the perpetually perplexed petty bourgeoisie that its interest lay in defending property against socialism. Once fascism was in power and the labour movement destroyed, capitalists no longer needed the fascist party, and so it was suppressed or marginalized.

This definition was not uncontested amongst Marxists. Some felt that it indiscriminately labelled all dictatorial regimes as fascist. Leon Trotsky preferred to differentiate 'Bonapartist' from fascist dictatorships. Bonapartism arose when there was a stalemate between workers and capitalists, in which neither could defeat the other, which permitted the state to govern temporarily. Such a regime was insufficiently powerful to destroy the left, and so was less dangerous than fascism.

Other Marxists felt that the petty bourgeoisie played a more autonomous role than the Communist International had allowed, and to some extent opposed the interests of capitalists. These criticisms were taken up by Marxists in the 1960s and 1970s in an effort to inject more flexibility into their model. Most Marxists did not, however, depart from the conviction that fascism operated 'ultimately' in the interests of capitalism. Those Marxists who did abandon the primacy of capitalist defence produced accounts not clearly differentiated from non-Marxist ones.

Marxist historians, often with great talent and imagination, have done much to illuminate the relationship between fascism and capitalism, and they have shown that the revolutionary discourse of fascists cannot be taken at face value. The strength of the Marxist approach is that it places fascism within the context of the wider social struggles of the 20th century.

Indeed, Marxist approaches deal almost exclusively in causes, and say less about how we could recognize a fascist movement – other than that it would take the form of a mass party recruited from the petty bourgeoisie, aspiring to dictatorship and denouncing both capitalism and socialism whilst in some way or other serving the interests of capitalism.

A major problem is that it is not saying very much to claim that fascism serves the interests of capitalism, because capitalism is such a powerful force in modern society that it can prosper under any regime that does not actually destroy it. Furthermore, whilst it can hardly be denied that capitalism conditions all sorts of social relationships, it is equally true that ideology, religion, and so on influence the way capitalists perceive their interests. So we must explain why some capitalists believed that fascism conformed to their interests, and others did not.

Neither does the power of capitalism mean that it is the 'ultimate' explanation of fascism. In trying to make it so, Marxists are forced to relegate much of fascism to secondary importance. In particular, the conviction that fascism must operate in capitalist interests or collapse obliges Marxists to play down the radical aspects of fascism. For Marxists socialism is the only genuine form of radicalism, so since fascists opposed socialism, they must have been reactionary. Marxists discount the fascist movement's radical opposition to the established administrative elite and mainstream politicians of both left and right, and their willingness to ignore the wishes of business where they seemed to obstruct the creation of a mobilized national community.

The necessity of proving that fascism ultimately serves capitalist interests also causes some Marxists to regard fascist territorial expansion and racism as a cunning plot to divert attention from the tensions between fascism's petty bourgeois and capitalist supporters, or merely as the technically most advanced of capitalism's crimes (an updated Highland clearance). Even if we accept the plausible contention that fascists appealed to nationalism partly in order to undermine workers' class loyalties, we still need to explain the mindset leading to the conviction that capitalist defence required such policies as the killing of the mentally ill in Nazi Germany or the Italianization of family names in South Tyrol. The possibility that these goals were pursued for reasons unrelated to the (supposed) logic of capitalism must be considered.

Fascism and antimodernism

The next theory to be considered is often known as 'Weberian', although its roots in the sociology of Max Weber (1864–1920) are not at all straightforward. Indeed, Marxist historians were primarily responsible for applying this theory to Spain and Italy. Nevertheless, the term 'Weberian' will be used for convention's sake.

Whereas Marxists held capitalists responsible for fascism, Weberians blamed the pre-industrial, or feudal, ruling class – the large landowners of Eastern Germany or the Italian Po Valley, the Latifundists of southern Spain, or the Japanese military caste. They argued that these elites were able to exert their baleful influence on the course of national histories because their countries had not experienced a genuine bourgeois and liberal-democratic revolution in the 19th century. These elites used education to spread their reactionary values through the rest of society, and resorted to ever more desperate means to preserve their positions. They sponsored mass nationalist movements in an attempt to undermine liberal democracy and socialism. German and Italian elites led their countries to war in 1914 in the hope that patriotic fervour would permit them to crush their domestic enemies. When this failed, they turned to fascism in a last-ditch attempt to destroy their enemies. Fascism was primarily an antimodern movement, resulting from the convergence of pre-industrial elites and the reactionary petty bourgeoisie.

The Weberian approach has enormously improved our understanding of fascism in its social context. It has shown that the old aristocracy, as much as capitalists, were immediately responsible for Hitler's accession to government in January 1933. There is no space here to engage in a detailed critique of this approach. Suffice it to say that it is not wholly convincing to regard fascism as 'antimodern', for it contained many allegedly 'modern' features too. Another difficulty is that the Weberian approach shares the Marxist assumption that the elites are able to manipulate the rest of the population – especially the petty bourgeoisie – almost at will. Like Marxism, Weberianism doesn't really account for the radical features of fascism. It pays more attention to fascist ideology than does Marxism, but reduces ideas to expressions of antimodernism.

Fascism as a form of totalitarian nationalism

The category of totalitarianism covers a diverse range of approaches to fascism, and is not wholly distinct from Weberianism, in that the latter sees the attempt to restore a pre-modern Utopia as a totalitarian project.

The word 'totalitarianism' was invented by Italian Fascists to encapsulate their drive to 'nationalize' the Italian masses – to incorporate them within a hierarchical, mobilized, militarized community serving the needs of Italy. As a scholarly idea the term enjoyed its heyday in the 1950s and 1960s, when anti-Marxist social scientists favoured a concept that discredited communism by linking it with fascism.

Famously, the American political scientist C. J. Friedrich defined totalitarianism as follows:

1. A single mass party, led by one man, which forms the hardcore of the regime and which is typically superior to or intertwined with the governmental bureaucracy.
2. A system of terror by the police and secret police which is directed against real and imagined enemies of the regime.
3. A monopolistic control of the mass media.
4. A near monopoly of weapons.
5. Central control of the economy.
6. An elaborate ideology which covers all aspects of man's existence and which contains a powerful chiliastic [messianic or religious] moment.

The final point is the most important, for fascists aim to restructure society in accordance with an ideological blueprint. Totalitarian theorists argue that in traditional societies a person's place in the world is dictated by divine plan. Modernization, however, causes the breakdown of religious certainties, and some people find this alarming (they suffer from what is termed cultural despair, angst, or anomie), so they create substitute 'religions' such as communism or fascism. Hannah Arendt argued that the essence of totalitarianism lay in the use of terror to make real an abstract ideological understanding of the world, and to destroy all existing human solidarities in the name of this programme.

In the 1970s the concept of totalitarianism fell out of use. The Cold War had thawed, and research demonstrated that, far from representing a 'top-down' system of control, Nazi and Fascist (and communist) regimes were characterized by unclear authority structures, and administrative chaos.

The collapse of communism in 1989 brought to light new evidence of the horrors of Stalinism, and gave totalitarianism a new lease of life. Meanwhile, the rise of postmodernism in Western universities revived scholars' interest in ideas. Postmodernists insist that we should analyse the internal structures of ideas, rather than see them as expressions of underlying economic, social, or other interests. Indeed, some postmodernists regard the belief in any fundamental organizing principle – be it God, class, nation, or race – as intrinsically oppressive, a view that converges neatly with totalitarian theory's view that fascism represents the attempt to create an ideal world according to absolute principles. Even those scholars who did not subscribe to the principles of postmodernism began once more to attend to fascists' ideas, especially their nationalism.

Many contemporary scholars see extreme nationalism as the core of fascist ideology. Roger Griffin argues that fascism is a form of 'populist ultranationalism' which aims to reconstruct the nation following a period of perceived crisis and decline – he uses the Victorian term 'palingenetic', meaning 'rebirth from the ashes', to characterize fascism. This attempted national resurrection is totalitarian in aspiration, if not achievement. Michael Burleigh, meanwhile, has brought back the idea of Nazism as a substitute religion.

For totalitarian theorists, fascist ideas are *revolutionary*, for to construct Utopia all existing structures must be levelled, whether parties, trade unions, families, or churches. Revolution also involves the creation of a 'new fascist man' – someone who lives only for the nation. Since real people are in fact diverse and far from perfectible, the only way to make them assume their places in Utopia is by force. Utopianism always leads to terror.

Contemporary proponents of the totalitarian thesis counter objections to earlier versions of the theory. They allow for the chaotic nature of totalitarian regimes. Indeed, they maintain that bureaucratic chaos helped create an *arbitrariness* in government which made it impossible for individuals to resist the regime. Totalitarianists also say that even if totalitarianism could not be achieved in practice, there was a *desire* to implement a Utopian programme. In a striking metaphor, Burleigh suggests that the Nazis sought to rebuild German society as engineers rebuild a bridge. They could not demolish it, since that would disrupt traffic, and therefore they replaced each individual part, so that passengers wouldn't notice.

Totalitarian theory demonstrates that ultranationalism is central to the fascist worldview, and that what fascists believe is important. Fascists' prioritization of the nation has radical implications, in that it potentially undermines family and property. Totalitarian theory also shows that fascism has much in common with religious fundamentalism, and that it pursues its goals with a violence justified by the conviction that opponents are part of a demonic conspiracy.

The weaknesses of totalitarian theory are the reverse of those of Marxist and Weberian approaches. Firstly, its one-sided preoccupation with ideas means that totalitarian theory is weak on the causes of fascism. Typically, it is content with mechanistic generalizations about the crisis of traditional ideas, a consequent sense of disorientation, and search for substitute religions. Thus defeat in the Great War, together with fear of revolution, is said to have bewildered the Germans and rendered them sympathetic to quasi-religious nationalist ideas which promised to restore the longed-for sense of certainty. Doubtless many were 'disorientated' in 1918. But there is no law that dictates that an upheaval of this nature *must* lead to disorientation. On the contrary, responses to crisis were diverse, and varied according to people's educational formation, social and religious position, age, and gender. One should not, therefore, seek the origins of fascist racial programmes, for instance, in a generalized sense of disorientation, but in the specific histories of specific groups, such as the medical profession, and one must ask how it was that those people who did espouse messianic forms of nationalism came to monopolize political power.

Second, totalitarian theory exaggerates the revolutionary side of fascism. It holds that a totalitarian regime aims to destroy *all* alternative solidarities in the drive to make all individuals equally dependent upon the regime and create a new society. Such a dream is actually impossible to *conceive*, let alone implement, for it requires an impossible impartiality. In reality, prejudices and unacknowledged assumptions shaped fascists' vision of their dystopia. Big business and the family (within certain limits) were more or less compatible with most fascists' perceptions of the mobilized nation. Communism and feminism were not. Totalitarianism is a useful concept only if we remember that it entails the urge to impose a worldview that is shaped by unconscious prejudices. So we should not expect the fascist Utopia to differ completely from the world as it presently exists – there lay the appeal of fascism for many.

Fascist nationalism also appears less revolutionary when we remember that it doesn't defend the rights of national groups in the name of a universal principle of equality for all individuals. Fascism contends that a nationality should restore its dominance or become dominant within a given state, and perhaps internationally too. Frequently fascist nationalism is that of the *dominant* ethnic group, or rather of a part of the dominant nationality which perceives itself, rightly or wrongly, to be neglected. In other cases fascism has appealed to ethnic groups that really are minorities – one thinks of Germans in Czechoslovakia in the 1930s. Here, fascists wanted to become part of another state where their own ethnic group was already dominant.

Defenders of the totalitarian approach respond to the criticism that their theory underplays the conservative impulses of fascism with the claim that compromises with conservatives are 'tactical', or they declare themselves, like Michael Burleigh, interested in 'fundamental psychology, rather than the surface of things' – an unconscious imitation of the Marxist method of dealing with recalcitrant facts.

To sum up, Burleigh's bridge metaphor is (inadvertently) useful in that it suggests that many believed that fascism would repair the nation whilst leaving them to get on with their lives. It is inadequate, however, because fascists endeavoured to reconstruct the bridge according to a substantially modified blueprint. Their project demanded the mobilization of enormous resources, shook the bridge to its foundations, and threatened to derail the rolling stock. Yet many passengers happily lent a hand and acclaimed the engineers. The latter, moreover, were convinced that other passengers were secretly plotting to blow up the bridge over which they were travelling. Our attention should not therefore be distracted from the scene in the trains passing over the bridge, where thugs were throwing fare-paying passengers into the ravine below, under the half-averted gaze of fellow travellers, who were perhaps wondering whether the murderers' uniforms were those of the usual guards. The totalitarian project is part novel, part familiar, and its realization depends on its appeal to particular groups and the amount of power and popular support available to them.

A definition

Our definition must incorporate the advantages of Marxist, Weberian, and totalitarian theories. It must not neglect either fascist ideas or their relationship with diverse social groups, and should account for both the radical and reactionary sides of fascism. And just as both radicalism and reaction are important, it follows that *all* elements of our definition of fascism are indispensable. I do not agree with Roger Griffin's view that we must distinguish between those elements of fascism that are specific to the inter-war period and therefore non-essential (he mentions the leader cult, paramilitarism, mass rallies, corporatist economics) and 'definitional traits', of which palingenetic ultranationalism is the most important. The trouble with this contention is that the nationalism espoused by fascists was as much a product of the inter-war period as was any other feature of the ideology. Nationalism was closely linked, for example, with paramilitarism and leader cult, for fascists believed the nation to be incarnate in the veterans and in the anointed leader. Fascism and its history would have been very different – as Chapters 4 and 5 will demonstrate – had a charismatic leader and mass party not claimed to incarnate the nation. Although fascists disagreed on the relative weight to be given to, and the meaning of, different aspects of fascism, all parts were linked together. If we see the features mentioned by Griffin as expendable, then we risk seriously misunderstanding the significance of fascism in the inter-war years, its internal dynamic, and how it differed from rival ideologies.

There have, of course, been many movements that have espoused some features of fascism and not others. Some of these can usefully be seen as belonging to a wider category of extreme right movements – by virtue of sharing an 'extreme' hostility to the left. Authoritarian conservative dictatorships, of which we shall meet several examples in subsequent chapters, provide one such example. An interesting case of a rather different type is the Parti social français, which flourished in France in 1936–9. This movement was descended from the fascistic Croix de feu, and retained its forerunner's nationalism and populism, yet differed in gradually abandoning paramilitarism, reducing its antidemocratic rhetoric, and increasingly becoming integrated into conventional electoral politics. Likewise, we shall see that contemporary movements, such as the British National Party and the French National Front, are certainly part of the extreme right, but are not fascist. Distinctions such as these might appear academic, but they are important because non-fascist extreme right movements do not have the same impact on the social and political system as fascist groups.

What form should our definition take? It is relatively easy to give a definition of fascism in list form. One could reel off characteristics such as ultranationalism, antisocialism, paramilitarism, nationalism, anticapitalism . . . Controversy begins when we attempt to elucidate the definition. What, for example, does 'anticapitalism' mean, given that fascists have not generally undermined big business? I prefer to advance a definition in the form of the continuous prose below, for it brings out the meaning of and linkages between the components, and the contradictory nature of fascism. The full significance of certain terms will become clearer in subsequent chapters.

Before proceeding, I should make clear that I cannot claim originality. My approach owes much to the earlier work of Ernesto Laclau, who still provides the best account of fascism in relation to the multiple conflicts present in modern society. My definition is also broadly compatible with Roger Eatwell's more recent work, which is particularly alive to the contradictions intrinsic to fascism. I have drawn too upon the methods and conclusions of recent historical research on the role of women and workers in fascist movements and regimes. These studies all show the complex interactions of fascists' ultranationalism with class, gender, religious, and other forms of identities, and they show that the binary oppositions usually used to classify fascism – such as modern and traditional, revolutionary and reactionary – require rethinking. Fascism is inherently contradictory.

Whilst fascism must be seen as an integrated set of ideas and practices, all of which are essential, intelligibility demands that we start somewhere, so I shall begin by accepting the 'new consensus' that fascism is a form of ultranationalist ideology and practice. This point of departure does not mean that nationalism is the 'core' from which all other aspects of fascism can be derived, or by which all aspects of fascism can be explained. It is impossible to say, for example, whether fascists opposed socialism because they saw it as a threat to national unity, or whether, conversely, they were nationalists primarily because they saw nationalism as an antidote to socialism. Neither does starting with ultranationalism entail uncritical acceptance of what fascists said about themselves, for we must remember that fascist ideology also comprised many unacknowledged ideas and assumptions. The focus on ultranationalism does, however, have the advantage of acknowledging the importance of fascists' *claim* to be nationalists above all else. Furthermore, Roger Griffin's view that fascism is an ideology that seeks to restore the nation after a period of supposed decline potentially captures the contradictory nature of an ideology that proposes change but also looks to the past.

Fascists, then, seek to create a mobilized national community, in which all sections of the population permanently demonstrate their love for the regime, and in which a 'new fascist man' would find fulfilment in service to the regime. The Nazis defined the nation biologically, others understood it culturally or historically. This nationalism need not be militarily expansionist. Some fascists, and even some Nazis, advocated a 'fascist international' of European, Western, Christian, Aryan, or white races. These 'international fascists' did not, however, deny that domestic policy should be determined by national principles. In Chapters 8, 9, and 10 I shall show how nationalism, intimately related to racial ideas, shaped fascist policies in areas such as welfare and family policy, as well as fascist views of relations between workers and employers and men and women.

Fascists condemn socialism, feminism, capitalism, and any other 'ism' on the grounds that these ideologies place some other criteria (class, gender, economic interest, and so on) above the nation. This is why fascism is so often described as a negative ideology – 'anti this' and 'anti that'. In fact, nationalism gives fascism a positive side too, allowing it to proclaim its superiority over mere 'sectional' interests. It is this absolute primacy of the nation that totalitarian theorists focus upon when they argue that fascism is revolutionary. Yet in our discussion of totalitarianism it was suggested that the fascist conception of the nation actually contains, alongside its revolutionary impulses, some more conventional ideas. Fascists see capitalism as more compatible with the national interest than socialism. When they spoke of creating a 'new man', they really did mean 'man', and their views of women were often rather conventional. Chapters 8, 9, and 10 will therefore also show that prejudices about class and gender *unconsciously* shaped fascists' nationalist priorities.

A good way to elucidate further the precise nature of fascism is to compare it with conservative dictatorships (such as the military regimes of inter-war Eastern Europe or Latin America). Authoritarian conservatives defended the primacy of a constellation of conservative 'interests': property, church, family, the military, the administration. They were highly nationalist, but believed that the elites, not the people, spoke for the nation, and their nationalism was moderated by the need to preserve the autonomy of conservative interests. So they left some space for private initiative: they did not completely abolish 'civil society' – the free association of individuals for economic, political, or other reasons. They made less attempt to regulate the family or the economy in the name of the national interest.

Fascism, in contrast, does not defend absolutely either property or family – both sacred to conservatives. Ultranationalism influences fascist attitudes towards property and family in three ways. Firstly, fascism discriminates between enterprises and families according to whether they belong to the favoured nationality. The property of 'foreigners' is sometimes expropriated; nationally (or racially) acceptable families are advantaged in the job market and the distribution of welfare benefits.

Secondly, without attacking capital *per se*, fascists argue that the 'selfishness' of big business (its pursuit of profit at the expense of harmony within the nation) impoverishes workers and drives them into the arms of socialism. Likewise, men and women's egoism is said to cause them to put comfortable living or careers before the production of healthy babies for the nation. These convictions permit what conservatives would see as legislative 'interference' by fascist regimes in economy and family. Businesses were subjected to regulation; workers were forced to join fascist unions; childbirth became a political duty. Authoritarian conservatives are uncomfortable with *any* attack on property – even Jewish property. Neither do conservatives, especially religious conservatives, like to see the family attacked in the name of the health of the nation.

Fascism also differs from authoritarian conservatism institutionally. The former governs through established bodies: churches, armies, and civil services. Authoritarian conservatives sometimes create mass organizations to provide support, but because they see family and business as the bulwarks of a private sphere free from state intervention, they do not seek to enrol mothers or workers in explicitly politicized organizations. Indeed, conservative dictatorships rarely suppress all existing non-political associations.

Fascists, in contrast, endeavour to bring to power a new elite at the head of a mass party, the latter being the embodiment of the people and the true source of national identity. The party seeks a monopoly on political representation and it tries to undermine the administrative, military, and church hierarchies on which conservatives rely – even if it doesn't always succeed. Whereas authoritarian conservatives use the police and army to suppress the left, fascist paramilitary organizations assume this task themselves, believing the authorities to be inadequate for the job. Fascists represent a new 'manly' elite invested with the task of replacing weak, 'effeminate', or 'impotent' established politicians, and ensuring that business and the family be subordinated to the national interest.

It is important to clarify what fascists mean when they appeal to the people. They do not see the people as an economic or social class – they do not, for example, mean the petty bourgeoisie. Rather, the term 'people' can be used to express the anti-establishment sentiments of *any* group – from discontented workers to wealthy capitalists. All we can say with certainty is that fascist supporters *see themselves as neglected by existing parties of both left and right* (whether they really are ignored is another matter). This feeling of abandonment reinforces fascist radicalism.

Furthermore, when fascists claim that the people's will must predominate over that of the corrupt elites, or when they describe existing governments as 'unrepresentative', they are not appealing to democracy as it is understood in liberal societies. Idealization of the people as the source of the new elite is mixed with contempt, for fascists insist on the unequal distribution of talents in individuals, and fear that without heroic leadership the masses will degenerate. The people are not capable of choosing a leader through the ballot box – elections simply permit the mediocre masses to choose mediocre representatives. Popular sovereignty must be expressed 'intuitively' through the fascist party and its leader. One of Codreanu's followers put it thus:

> there must be a creative element in history that is neither the man against the masses ([conservative] dictatorship) nor the masses against the man (the degenerate democracy of our time), but the man whom the masses have found.
>
> *Cuvintul*, 27 January 1938

Historically, fascist movements have emerged from two sources. In the inter-war years disaffected supporters of right-wing parties provided most, although not all, fascist recruits – we shall see this in Chapters 4, 5, and 6. In crisis conditions many rank-and-file conservatives felt that the traditional right was too feeble to achieve national unity or deal with socialism, feminism, economic crisis, and international difficulties. They saw fascists as more patriotic and determined than traditional conservatives. In effect, they regarded elimination of the establishment as the precondition for the restoration of order. They demanded order in the name of revolution, and revolution in the name of order.

Fascism can also emerge from a crisis of the left. This was rare, but not unknown, in the inter-war years, but is more pronounced in the present. When fascism derives from the left, its distinctive combination of radicalism and reaction comes from the combination of residual leftist hostility to the establishment with the feeling that the left has betrayed the people – for example, by excessive attention to ethnic minorities or feminists. Of course, not all of those who reject established parties turn to fascism.

The diverse origins of those who became fascists underlines, once again, the contradictory nature of fascism, and reminds us that fascists disagreed amongst themselves about the very essence of their movement. Some placed more emphasis on fascism's radical aspects, others on its conservative side (a few embraced only the radical or reactionary sides, but from our point of view they ceased to be properly fascist, whatever they claimed). There were also disagreements about the nature of fascism's radicalism. Some saw it as residing in its corporatist approach to labour relations, while others believed that corporatism undermined the primacy of the national interest. A minority saw fascism as an opportunity to advance the cause of women, while the majority saw fascism as a sort of 'manly revolution'. Further disputes were caused by fascism's relationship with conservatism. Given fascists' desire to restore order and destroy the left, it was always likely to attract support from authoritarian conservatives. Yet fascists also wanted to supplant conservatives as the embodiment of the nation. Fascists rarely broke entirely with conservatism, but relations were always difficult.

Fascism is indelibly marked by the specific context of inter-war Europe – the legacy of the Great War and the intellectual agendas (especially the tendency to depict human society and relations between states in terms of laws of nature and by the search for a 'third way' between capitalism and socialism) and social conflicts of that period. Nevertheless, once created, fascism becomes an 'available ideology' potentially capable of deployment in quite different circumstances. It is not impossible that it could reappear in largely unmodified form.

Fascism is a set of ideologies and practices that seeks to place the nation, defined in exclusive biological, cultural, and/or historical terms, above all other sources of loyalty, and to create a mobilized national community. Fascist nationalism is reactionary in that it entails implacable hostility to socialism and feminism, for they are seen as prioritizing class or gender rather than nation. This is why fascism is a movement of the *extreme* right. Fascism is also a movement of the *radical* right because the defeat of socialism and feminism and the creation of the mobilized nation are held to depend upon the advent to power of a new elite acting in the name of the people, headed by a charismatic leader, and embodied in a mass, militarized party. Fascists are pushed towards conservatism by common hatred of socialism and feminism, but are prepared to override conservative interests – family, property, religion, the universities, the civil service – where the interests of the nation are considered to require it. Fascist radicalism also derives from a desire to assuage discontent by accepting specific demands of the labour and women's movements, so long as these demands accord with the national priority. Fascists seek to ensure the harmonization of workers' and women's interests with those of the nation by mobilizing them within special sections of the party and/or within a corporate system. Access to these organizations and to the benefits they confer upon members depends on the individual's national, political, and/or racial characteristics. All aspects of fascist policy are suffused with ultranationalism.

The above definition is relatively full. It does not have to explain away aspects that do not fit as 'tactical', or claim that certain parts are 'ultimately' the most important. It covers both fascist ideas and their contexts. It accounts for radical as well as reactionary features of fascism, and indeed sees these as intimately related. Fascism's ambiguity explains why it is both attracted to and repelled by conservatism, and makes sense of the oft-noted oscillations between radicalism and reaction in fascism's history. Despite some attempts to see the history of fascism in terms of a series of definable 'stages', there was no clear pattern to fascism's frequent changes of direction. Its mutations resulted from conflicts within fascist movements operating in unpredictable historical circumstances, which will be explored in subsequent chapters.

I cannot make exaggerated claims for this definition. If I wished to examine common ideological structures in Stalinism and Nazism, the concept of totalitarianism would be more appropriate. If my purpose was to explain the Holocaust, only a range of concepts, including fascism, totalitarianism, and capitalism, would enable me to grasp what was both unique and general about it. I can only suggest that this definition is the best available for the specific purpose of this little book, which is to examine fascism in its social, cultural, and political context.

Chapter 3
Fascism before fascism?

Fascism was a product of the Great War and the crisis that followed. Nevertheless, premonitions of fascism appeared in the decades before 1914 – none of them quite the full-blown thing. The first anticipation of fascism may have emerged in Tennessee shortly after the American Civil War, when demobilized Confederate officers set up the Ku Klux Klan (KKK) to defend the supremacy of the white race against the government's perceived partiality towards blacks. The KKK wore special dress, engaged in bizarre rituals designed to underline their membership of a distinctive community, and murdered blacks in the name of a law 'from which no human laws can permanently derogate'. Membership might have reached half a million before the Klan was disbanded by its leaders in 1869. A second wave of organization began in 1915, stimulated partly by D. W. Griffith's silent movie *The Birth of a Nation*, which portrayed the first KKK as the saviour of America. Although the KKK anticipated many features of fascism, not least its racism, it was also differentiated from fascism by a degree of anti-state, libertarian, populist individualism which has always characterized large parts of the American extreme right. For more genuine precursors of fascism we must look to Europe. Even there, ultranationalism lacked important features of fascism, and it was stronger in France, where fascism never achieved power, than it was in Germany or Italy.

Before the Great War conservative parties were largely controlled by the wealthy few – some were little more than politicized gentlemen's clubs. The new radical right, which emerged in the late 1880s and 1890s, appealed, in contrast, to the people. A number of converging intellectual, political, social, and economic developments made this possible. In what follows I shall emphasize the radical right's tendency to borrow from all parts of the political spectrum ideas and practices which at the time were usually considered to be incompatible.

Let us begin with fascism's intellectual origins. If we define fascism narrowly enough it can be traced back to the radical sects of the Reformation or even the classical world. This would be fruitful were our purpose to study an intolerant, illiberal, quasi-religious mindset. But since we want to enquire into the common characteristics of certain movements and regimes in recent history, a more useful starting point is the 18th century, for it produced something akin to modern political alignments.

The 18th-century inheritance is nevertheless complex. On the one hand, fascism owed something to the Enlightenment idea that society need not be determined by tradition, but could be organized according to a blueprint derived from universal principles. The Enlightenment thinker Jean-Jacques Rousseau's notion that society should be governed by one such universal ideal, the 'general will', is especially relevant, since it was taken up by the most revolutionary of the French Revolutionaries, the Jacobins. The Jacobins justified violence as a means to construct a new order and weed out those who opposed the general will (or the nation). They were ready to force people to be free.

On the other hand, fascism owes a debt to anti-Enlightenment thought. Many German opponents denied the validity of universal principles in the name of national traditions. French counter-revolutionaries, such as Joseph de Maistre, contended that 'natural' communities – nation, profession, and family – were more important than the individual. Anti-Enlightenment philosophy had a great influence on 19th-century Romanticism, which repudiated reason in favour of nature worship, and counterpoised the genius of the artist to mass mediocrity.

Narrowing the focus, some have situated the emergence of the radical right in the context of the revolt against reason, said to characterize the last decades of the 19th century. There is something in this, but proto-fascism was not irrationalist in a simple sense. Certainly, many *fin de siècle* thinkers opposed rationalism and its ramifications: liberalism, socialism, materialism, individualism. They were pessimists, who refused to see history in terms of progress, and instead saw it as a desperate struggle against degeneration. The fascist call for an elite to save the nation from degeneration – the idea of rebirth from the ashes – emanated from this climate.

In Germany various strands of spiritualist thought, descended from Romanticism, informed the idea of the German people – the *volk* – as an ethical, socially united, patriarchal, ethnic, and linguistic community. In France, Barrès attacked rationalist republicanism in the name of a cult of ancestors and the soil. Amongst those who influenced fascists one could also cite another French thinker, Gustave Le Bon, who argued that irrational crowds were manipulated by charismatic leaders, and Georges Sorel, who argued likewise that the masses were motivated by myths. The Italian political scientists Gaetana Mosca and Vilfredo Pareto emphasized the role of force in politics. The German philosopher Friedrich Nietzsche was convinced that universalism had undermined respect for the strong. He hoped that a man of destiny would create a more spiritual community. Scholars have disagreed about the extent to which these great thinkers were themselves proto-fascist. The nub is that their ideas were appropriated and misappropriated by proto-fascists.

MAURICE BARRÈS

2. Maurice Barrès in 1888. Late 19th-century dress codes made it difficult for nationalist intellectuals to pose as men of the people.

Proto-fascists drew on contemporary science (or rather pseudo-science) as well as irrationalism. Darwin's principle of the survival of the fittest was, and remains, respectable in scientific terms, but its application to social policy was more dubious. Social Darwinists feared that the comforts of modern society, coupled to assistance to the poor, would lead to social degeneration and decadence. They preached 'eugenicism' as the answer, proposing 'negative' measures such as sterilization of the unfit, and/or 'positive' reforms such as encouragement of reproduction of the healthy. Some Social Darwinists felt that only strong leaders could prevent the masses from succumbing to a late 19th-century equivalent of couch-potato syndrome. Social Darwinists also believed that there was a struggle for domination between nation-states. Some felt that the fate of individuals was of little import compared to that of the nation.

Social Darwinism was allied to the even more questionable 'science' of race. The French monarchist Count Gobineau's 'Essay on the Inequality of Human Races', ignored since publication in 1853, began, regrettably, to be read in the 1890s. One admirer was the composer Richard Wagner, who blended antisemitism, Germanic Christianity purged of its 'Jewish elements', and paganism into an idealized Germanic myth. His son-in-law, Houston Stewart Chamberlain, added fashionable 'scientific' Social Darwinist and racist ideas. Hitler was a devotee of Chamberlin, and spent his life dreaming Wagnerian dreams of victory or death. Hitler denied, none-theless, that Nazism was a religion – some of his speeches read like parodies of the dogmatic turgidity perfected by 'scientific socialists'.

It is appealing, but facile, to draw direct lines between this cultural climate and fascism, for fascism was only one of many possible consequences. Eugenicism, for instance, was invented in Britain by the conservative Francis Galton and his left-wing pupil Karl Pearson. Proto-fascism was part of a huge range of ideas, including mysticism and scientism, traditionalism and modernism, reason and unreason. Some nationalists looked back to a rural paradise, while the Italian Futurists celebrated the machine age.

If we really want to explain how ideas such as these became embodied in proto-fascist and fascist movements, we must attend to context. To start with, this period saw the emergence of modern disciplines in the universities: history, sociology, political science, physics, biology, literary criticism, and so on. The rise of professional, specialized research led to displacement of old-style scholars, sometimes amateurs, who claimed expertise in several fields. Lawyers and doctors, who had previously dominated university faculties, were especially likely to pretend to wide competence, and were attracted to the racist, eugenicist, psychological, and historical ideas described above.

These polymaths often resented their lack of recognition from specialist professional academics, and compensated by seeking political success. Some favoured the extreme left (the legally trained Lenin was a quintessential generalist); others the new right. Barrès gave the republican establishment's refusal to honour a now-forgotten race theorist as a reason for entering politics. It is no accident that doctors and lawyers were prominent in the far right. Their resentment of specialists was coupled with fear that professions were overcrowded with Jews and women, and with dislike of government plans to introduce 'socialist' health-care programmes. Doctors and lawyers espoused eugenicist theories, which they thought gave them the right to play god. Specialist academics were often just as influenced by pseudo-scientific knowledge and nationalism. In pre-war ultranationalist movements specialists sometimes held sway, but generalists with chips on their shoulders increasingly set the agenda.

This was all the more significant given that it was within the framework of eugenics and racism that many of the elites confronted the advance of democracy at the turn of the century – the much feared 'age of the masses'. Racist and eugenicist ideas represented, for some, a new, more effective means to govern and control the dangerous masses. All over Europe, from progressive France to autocratic Russia, entitlement to the vote had been extended before 1914 (not usually to women). Public interest in elections grew, while mass nationalist, socialist, Catholic, and peasant parties emerged. Alongside them sprouted multitudinous single-issue groups, from vegetarian societies to trade unions, women's groups, and colonialist lobbies. Permanent national organizations were made possible by technological advance. Railways spread from major routes to smaller localities. The telephone and typewriter began to have an impact. Without the vote and the technical means to organize in a democratic society, fascism could not have existed.

This was also a period of imperialism. The carve-up in the 1880s and 1890s of Africa and much of Asia by the great powers stimulated national rivalries and promoted racism. Italian and German belief that they had not gained their fair share of empire provoked nationalist hysteria, while defence of huge empires was essential to British and French ultranationalists. European powers drew upon contemporary racist science to justify domination over non-European peoples. Judgements about the 'characters' of members of 'inferior' races permitted colonial powers to disregard the rule of law where they thought it appropriate. Near-exterminationist policies practised against some native peoples provided, with hindsight, precedents for the Holocaust.

Nationalism, too, flourished. At this time national separatists were liberals, democrats, and/or socialists. Since they challenged the ruling classes of the multinational Russian, Habsburg, and British states, they presented their demands in terms of equal treatment for all nationalities (although in some cases universalism was a thin veneer). Nevertheless, some nationalists espoused a potentially undemocratic form of romantic nationalism, which required quasi-mystical daily affirmation of the national idea by all inhabitants. For instance, in the 1890s many Polish nationalists broke with liberalism and prioritized 'will'. They believed that xenophobia, aggression, and violence would make the Polish nation.

Proto-fascism was strong in countries where nationalist movements had recently established new states – Germany and Italy especially. Governments in these countries set about turning mere subjects into national citizens through education, linguistic conformity, conscription, and limitation of the influence of supranational churches. The recently established French Republic was just as keen to turn its peasant population into Frenchmen. These state's policies exacerbated competition for jobs, reward, and education between ethnic groups within these states – as in the saltworks of Aigues-Mortes.

Radical-right movements also emerged where ruling nationalities were threatened by separatist movements. In the Austrian part of the Austro-Hungarian Empire, the dominant Germans felt that too much had been conceded to Czechs and Poles. In Russia after the Revolution of 1905 radical nationalist movements emerged, as they did in Britain during the Irish Home Rule Crisis of 1911–14.

Antisocialism was a further ingredient in the pre-fascist soup. In the 1890s and 1900s socialist parties broke into mass politics in many countries, including Russia, Austria, Germany, France, and Italy, while strikes, often political, spread across Europe and America. In parallel with these socialist parties, and often in reaction against them, a whole host of antisocialist organizations sprang up, including anti-Marxist trade unions, artisan associations, peasant leagues, and business groups. These bodies often overlapped in terms of membership and organization with nationalist movements.

The appearance of feminism as an organized movement represented another aspect of organized politics and mass society. Feminism was strongest in America and Britain, but was present to a greater or lesser degree in most European countries. In the 1890s feminists became increasingly vociferous in their demands for access to the professions, and in the following decade turned their attention to the vote in some countries. Right-wing popular associations were in the forefront of the inevitable male backlash.

The radical right did not, then, derive from ultranationalism or extreme antisocialism alone. It was a diffuse reaction, rooted in daily struggles for jobs, financial reward, educational success, and political honour against socialists, ethnic minorities, feminists, and liberals in a context of imperialism and nation-building. Thus in Germany, radical right associations included the explicitly nationalist Pan-Germans, a League of Struggle Against the Emancipation of Women, and an Imperial League Against Social Democracy. For ultranationalists everywhere, all such threats to the nation were connected. Socialism represented a danger to property, nation, and male power in the family. Jews were blamed for corrupting the nation, and promoting feminism and socialism. Feminists and socialists were the agents of Judaism. The radical right saw its enemies as part of a demonic conspiracy.

The radical right was not convinced that the established right was fit to deal with the danger, and it was true that governments, fearful of stirring up mass hysteria, often soft-pedalled national issues. The radical right called for governments more responsive to the needs of the people. German radical nationalists condemned 'courtly Byzantinism', and demanded 'the elevation of all parts of the nation to consultation and participation in national matters' – paradoxically through a strong leader.

In political terms, this populism emerged from the convergence of three strands. Firstly, it represented a distorted descendant of an older tradition of European democratic radicalism which had climaxed in the Revolutions of 1848. Democratic radicalism, whilst considerably more generous than the radical right would be, had never been entirely humanitarian. It had rarely favoured rights for women, and had sometimes been xenophobic. This exclusionary subcurrent became more pronounced in the late 19th century, in a context of imperialism, nationalism, antifeminism, and antisocialism. The emergence of feminism brought out the implicit misogyny of popular radicalism. The rise of Marxist socialism in particular pushed popular radicalism to the right (not all elements, it must be stressed). Traditional radicalism had demanded rights for the 'people' and the 'nation', categories that included wage earners, small masters, shopkeepers, and peasants. Marxism, however, largely appealed to industrial workers alone, and was internationalist. There are many instances of this shift from left to right: the composer Richard Wagner had fought on the barricades in 1848; shopkeepers in Paris and Vienna moved from radicalism to the xenophobic right.

Secondly, universal suffrage, coupled with social and economic developments, permitted the mobilization in the radical right of hitherto quiescent rank-and-file conservatives. In some French and Italian rural areas, Catholic priests (once regarded as bulwarks of the established order) stirred up the peasantry. In Germany parish-pump politicians depicted socialists, Junkers (the aristocracy), and Jews as enemies of the peasantry.

Thirdly, many cases of elite support for the radical right could be invoked – British conservatives connived with Carson's Ulster Volunteers; Prussian Junkers founded the German Land League; French royalists funded the Antisemitic League during the Dreyfus Affair. This backing was motivated partly by the recognition that old and new rights shared hostility to feminism, socialism, and national minorities. Yet a degree of elite defensiveness was also present, for in this period many conservatives felt that the 'rise of the masses' was an inevitable process with which conservatives must compromise or risk political death. They therefore allied with the radical right *despite* its radical tendencies, in the hope that they could divert demands for greater democracy into the lesser evil of authoritarian populism. The actual history of proto-fascist movements was determined by the interaction, in specific national contexts, of elite and radical groups.

France provided the most favourable terrain in pre-war Europe for proto-fascism. It had been defeated by Germany in 1870, and had the worst of imperial conflicts with Britain. Revolution had been notoriously frequent in France, and now Marxist socialism and revolutionary trade unionism seemed to threaten new upheavals. Republican governments, with considerable success, endeavoured to construct a unitary national state on liberal-democratic principles, but faced serious resistance from Catholics. France's need for immigrants to work in its new large factories stimulated popular xenophobia.

The French radical right resulted from the meeting of three tendencies: royalists marginalized and radicalized by successive defeats at the hands of republicans; Catholic populists desperate to resist secularization and capture leadership of the proletariat from the socialists; and nationalists annoyed by the government's apparent lack of interest in revenge against Germany. Socially, the radical right appealed to *déclassé* aristocrats like the antisemitic Marquis de Morès, racist shopkeepers in Paris, and xenophobic workers who flocked to 'Yellow' trade unions during the 1900s.

Italy was unified between 1859 and 1870 through military action by the state of Piedmont and its French ally, rather than by a broadly based nationalist movement. Some nationalists therefore felt that Italy had not been truly unified, a view apparently confirmed by the narrow political base of Italy's pre-1914 Liberal governments. The franchise was limited, and Catholics refused to participate in elections because unification had been achieved at the expense of the Pope's rule over central Italy. Furthermore, in the 1890s Italy had experienced parliamentary scandals, working-class unrest in the north, occupation of landed estates by poor peasants in the south, military defeat in Abyssinia in 1896, and the assassination of the king in 1900.

Convinced that repression was not working, the left liberal Giovanni Giolitti, prime minister from 1901, set about wooing moderate socialists and Catholics to his government. Giolitti had some success, but could not prevent the mobilization of the radical right against him. Nationalists felt that Giolitti further undermined national unity by pandering to socialists. In 1910 nationalists came together in the Italian Nationalist Association (INA). This association received support from big business, the administration, and academics, but recruited largely from the middle classes, including lawyers and especially teachers, of whom the future philosopher of fascism Giovanni Gentile was one. Teachers were in the forefront of the struggle to 'make' Italians.

The INA evoked the great 19th-century patriot Mazzini's nationalism, yet stripped it of its liberal humanism, and preached that national unity could be achieved only by an authoritarian state. This entailed suppression of socialist organizations and incorporation of workers into new corporatist bodies, loyal to the Italian nation. The INA also wanted to refashion the nation through war. The intellectual Enrico Corradini called for 'feminine' liberal internationalism to give way to 'male' virility. He didn't see war as a means to precise foreign-policy objectives, or to obtain markets and raw materials, but to integrate all classes into the mobilized nation.

There was, moreover, some convergence between the INA and revolutionary syndicalists (who believed that trade unions should lead the march towards socialism). Some syndicalist intellectuals had become convinced by the failure of strike movements that socialism was impossible in contemporary Italy. They held that a genuine national state had to be created before the proletariat could take power, and agreed with nationalists that war might help achieve this objective. In any case, syndicalists had believed in 'the people' more than the proletariat, and they were influenced by the eugenicist ideas and cultural climate described above.

Germany, too, had been unified in 1866 to 1871 'from above', thanks to Prussian armies. The nation was founded upon elitist conservative nationalism marked by anti-Catholicism, antisocialism, antifeminism, and antiliberalism. Ultranationalism flourished in this climate. Julius Langbehn's anonymously published *Rembrandt as Educator* (1890) was a perfect example of *völkisch* output. Langbehn believed that the Dutch master, like his fellow countrymen, was actually German by race, and his chaotic book depicted Rembrandt as the teacher of a new German reformation. Langbehn epitomized amateur generalists – he nourished a life-long grievance against the 'dissipation' of science into specialization. He advocated combining science with art, and replacing dry professional history with a history informed by the psychic reality of race. He evoked both contemporary eugenic science (holding that if Berlin bars were replaced by public baths, socialism would be washed away) and, like Wagner, he evoked the myth of the artist-hero, rooted in the *volk*, who would complete political unity with spiritual. Langbehn's new reformation required suppression of political divisions, revival of more 'virile' (and heretical) Germanic Christianity, treatment of Jews as 'poison', and the establishment of a German empire from Amsterdam to Riga. Langbehn's book sold enormously well. Even Catholics welcomed its critique of progressive ideas, despite Langbehn's blasphemous views and identification of Germany with the Protestant peasantry. In the late 1920s sales of Langbehn's work took off again.

In the 1890s this *völkisch* programme was taken seriously by many conservatives, who shared the ultranationalists' enemies and harnessed nationalist demagogy to the defence of material interest. Conservative landowners sponsored the populist, antisocialist, and antisemitic Land League to win peasant support for protectionist tariffs, while the Eastern Marches Society agitated for the conquest of new agricultural land in the east at the expense of Poles. Business interests, wealthy professionals, and government officials sponsored the Pan-German League and the Navy League in the belief that colonialism represented a means to consolidate the German state and provide markets for industry.

Popular nationalism mattered too in Germany. The Agrarian League had been built partly from pre-existing peasant associations, such as the groups led by Otto Böckel, the 'King of the Peasants', which blamed Jews, cities, priests, doctors, the state, and even the aristocracy for their problems. At its Tivoli conference in 1893, the German Conservative Party incorporated antisemitism into its platform in the hope of defusing this discontent. When the highly conservative government launched its naval building campaign in 1896 it relied for propaganda upon the Pan-German League. Yet this league became considerably more radical than the government, particularly in its attacks on Catholics and British policy. By 1902, under the leadership of Heinrich Claβ, the Pan-Germans shifted their loyalty from the Kaiser to the *volk*. In 1913 Claβ argued that only a strong leader could save Germany, a programme summed up in his pamphlet *If I were Kaiser*.

Austrian radical nationalism was closely related to German. The Austrian part of the Habsburg Empire was organized along unique lines. A semi-absolutist Germanic dynasty and bureaucracy presided over a federation of national groups possessed of considerable rights. Inevitably, the dominant Germans felt that the government sacrificed their interests to minorities, especially the nearly autonomous Hungarians and the Czechs. The most important radical nationalist movement – Karl Lueger's Christian Social Party – emerged in Vienna, a hotchpotch of ethnic rivalries and the headquarters of a powerful socialist movement. Lueger, originally favourable to the liberal-democratic left, won support from Viennese artisans, white-collar workers, and teachers, who resented 'Jewish' capitalism and socialism, and their own exclusion from the bourgeoisie. At first the movement's radical antisemitism and Catholic social doctrine frightened the old right – Emperor Franz-Joseph refused to approve Lueger's election as mayor of Vienna for two years. Subsequently, Lueger became more moderate, and allied with rural conservatives. This cleared space for more radical groups, such as the Ostara Society, which sought to purify the Aryan race of contamination by racial inferiors, liberals, and socialists. Hitler, then one of Vienna's many aimless poor, was a reader of Ostara tracts.

During the 1905 Revolution, Russian conservatives too reacted against the upsurge of ethnic minorities. The Union of the Russian

People – better known as the Black Hundreds – was sponsored by the administration and Tsar, who shared the delusion that the revolution was the work of Jews. With the connivance of the authorities, the Black Hundreds contributed to hundreds of pogroms, in which over 3,000 Jews were murdered. Notwithstanding collaboration with the old right, the Black Hundreds were appalled by the Tsar's apparent inability to deal with the left, and wished to install a 'popular autocracy'.

Before 1914 British conservatism included ultranationalist elements. The triumph of the Liberals in 1906, and their repeated election victories in following years, left the Conservative Party bitterly divided. Meanwhile, Liberal social reforms, the reduction in the powers of the House of Lords, the rise of Labour, and strikes and suffragette demonstrations provoked fears of revolution. The passage of an Irish Home Rule Act seemed to presage the break-up of the United Kingdom. Ulster's resistance to Irish Home Rule stimulated radical nationalism there, and many Conservatives sympathized with it. Some accused German-Jewish financiers of plundering the nation, while in London's East End a Brothers League with 45,000 members attacked Jews seeking refuge from pogroms in Russia.

Finally, the Hungarian case shows that not all manifestations of intolerant nationalism were right-wing. Hungary had achieved autonomy within the Habsburg monarchy in 1867, and had embarked on a programme of Magyarization of national minorities and reduction of the influence of the Catholic Church. Opposition Magyar nationalists nevertheless demanded greater vigour in the construction of the national state. They resented the role of the Austrian dynasty in Hungarian affairs, ethnic minorities' resistance to Magyarization, and the spread of internationalist socialism in Budapest. Extracted from their context, these ideas prefigured fascism – all the more so as nationalists wanted to resurrect Hungary after a period of alleged decline. Yet opposition nationalists in Hungary remained on the left, for the right wanted closer union with Austria – an anathema to the nationalists. Although Hungarian nationalism fed into fascism after the war, it was for the moment separated from the radical right by a thoroughgoing opposition to conservatives.

Even where radical-right movements did emerge, they weren't always direct precursors of fascism. Studies of Germany show that there was no clear correlation between support for antisemites in the 1890s and backing for the Nazis. The radical right was weaker than in France, where fascism never triumphed. Had it not been for Mussolini and Hitler, pre-war ultranationalists in Italy and Germany might have been regarded as historical curiosities. None of the movements examined, except perhaps in France, wanted power in their own right. More often they sought to radicalize existing regimes. Above all, they were dominated more than fascist movements by the established elites – big business, professional academics, religious leaders, and bureaucrats. The most we can say is that radical nationalism had become one of the options available to the extreme right all over Europe, and might be utilized in crisis conditions. Moreover, radical nationalism was only one of several potential forms of populist protest, which might be directed against Jews or other minorities, capitalists, and/or socialists. The victory of fascism in Italy and Germany was not, therefore, predetermined before 1914.

The Great War

The Great War, the peace treaties, and the economic difficulties of the inter-war years fundamentally changed the situation. Established conservatism was weakened, for beleaguered governments made substantial concessions to nationalists, peasants, socialists, and women in a bid to win support for war efforts. As the war ended, popular discontent and uprisings all over Europe caused frightened governments to reinforce democracy and grant increased rights to women, workers, and ethnic minorities. The Russian Revolution provoked immense fear in conservative

Europe, especially as communist movements sprouted in Hungary, Finland, France, and Germany. Not only did communism promise the destruction of capitalism, but of the family, and it took up the cause of ethnic minorities all over Europe.

Inevitably a reaction developed against these many-headed threats. Given the discredit of existing conservative movements, reaction was often led by the new right. This happened, moreover, in a climate brutalized by war and civil war, and in which nationalism had been greatly boosted. Governments became preoccupied with ensuring that their nation was fit to survive in the difficult international situation of the post-war world. Wartime governments had intervened in economic, social, and family life to an extent never before seen in Europe, and this encouraged many to think that science and state planning could restore national greatness. In its most radical form, adopted by fascists everywhere, national strength implied economic self-sufficiency behind tariff walls, repression of socialism and incorporation of the workers into the national community, encouragement of women to abandon careers and equality in favour of having babies for the nation, assimilation or expulsion of ethnic minorities, and the introduction of eugenic social welfare schemes designed to improve the physical fitness of the nation.

War also encouraged the use of force for political ends. Not all old soldiers worshipped force – many became pacifists. Yet the appearance of paramilitary movements all over Europe in the inter-war years was clearly a product of the war. It is, in fact, impossible to understand fascism without taking into account the upheaval of the Great War. So important was it that fascism has struggled to impose itself outside the temporal and geographical context of inter-war Europe.

Chapter 4
Italy: 'making history with the fist'

Benito Mussolini first came to national attention in 1912 as the leader of the Italian Socialist Party's radical wing, opposed to cooperation with Giolitti and his Libyan war. True to his left-wing principles, Mussolini initially advocated that Italy remain neutral in the Great War. Yet in 1915 he joined the politically diverse Interventionist movement, where he met Futurists, radical nationalists, and conservative Liberals. From 1915 Mussolini sided with the nationalists amongst his new friends, henceforth regarding nation as a more potent political force than class. But Mussolini never lost his moral dislike for the political or business establishments. He was influenced by revolutionary syndicalists, and like them became convinced that nationalism would produce a movement able to have done with bourgeois liberalism and forge a new Italy.

In 1915 the Interventionists had their way, and Italy entered the war. War did change Italy, but it didn't create the national unity dreamed of by nationalists. On the contrary, the war exacerbated class and gender conflict. The Socialist Party maintained its opposition to the war throughout – unlike any of its European counterparts. Levels of unionization grew and strikes were numerous. Over 600,000 men were killed and demoralization spread through the army. The war also seemed to invert normal relations between the sexes, for women had taken over some male jobs and were believed to have become more interested in profiting from the absence of menfolk than in aiding the war effort.

Defeat at Caporetto in October 1917 belatedly galvanized public opinion, permitting Italy to hold out for the rest of the war. In the peace treaty much territory was won from Austria, though inevitably not as much as the unassuageable nationalists wanted. Outraged, the poet D'Annunzio, at the head of a band of veterans, seized the Adriatic port of Fiume in September 1919, and was not expelled until the end of the following year. Nationalist anger at the 'mutilated victory' was exacerbated by continued social unrest. In 1918–20 (the 'Red Years') strikes with factory occupations were common in the cities of the north, while in the Po Valley, agricultural labourers and peasants engaged in strikes, and in the south landless labourers occupied uncultivated land. In border regions Slav and German minorities demanded autonomy. The women's movement, too, had been stimulated by involvement in the war effort, and the lower house of parliament approved women's suffrage, although the measure did not become law. In the general elections of 1919, Socialist and Catholic parties made major gains. But since neither could govern alone, and neither would join a coalition with the other, the old Liberal politicians formed a series of administrations with Catholic support. These were paralysed by divisions between followers and opponents of Giolitti, interventionists, and neutralists.

This was the context in which fascism became a mass movement. Hitherto Mussolini had been irrelevant. His *Fascio di Combattimento*, founded in Milan on 23 March 1919, recruited a few ex-soldiers, syndicalists, and Futurists. Its programme combined nationalism with republicanism, anticlericalism, female suffrage, and social reform, the guiding idea being the mobilization of men and women, workers and employers, peasants and landowners in a secular national community. Fascism polled hardly

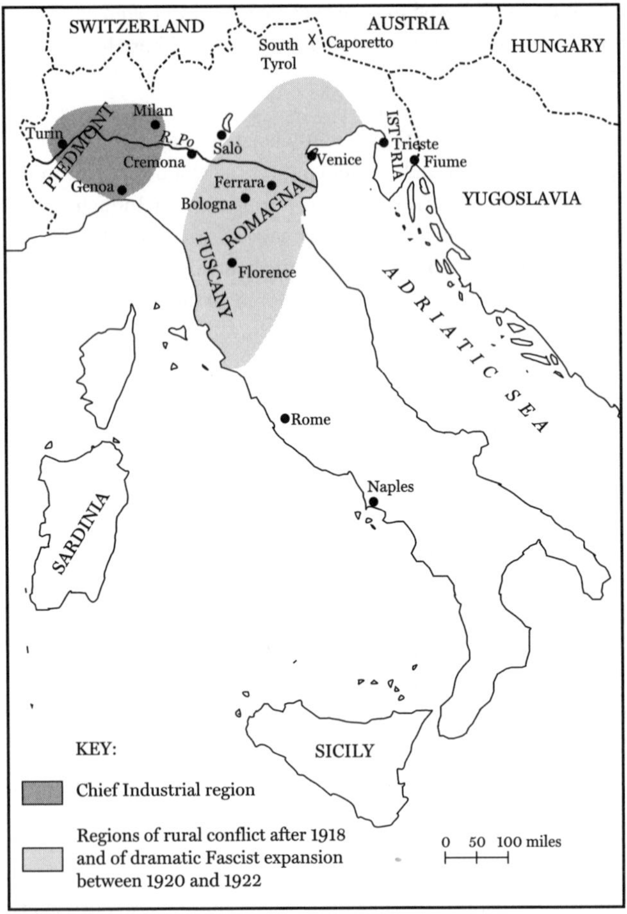

Map 2. Italy

any votes in 1919, but in 1921, as working-class and peasant
agitation reached its peak, it began to win recruits.

Fascism took off in regions affected by agrarian unrest, where the
youthful rural bourgeoisie began to join in large numbers. These

sons of estate managers, small-town officials, and teachers, many of them veterans, saw in fascism a means to take upon themselves the task of fighting the Socialist and Catholic leagues. They won the support of many conservative small peasants and landless labourers, who agreed that the authorities were not protecting them from the left. Fascist squads (*squadristi*) began a violent campaign of intimidation against Catholics and especially Socialists, in which many hundreds were killed. By 1922 the Fascists had effectively taken over the administration of law and order in many rural areas. Meanwhile Fascists fought with Slav minorities in the Venezia Giulia, and expanded in the cities, where they helped break a general strike in July. By the end of 1922 Fascism possessed a quarter of a million members.

Large landowners and big businessmen, who despaired of government support against strikers, provided encouragement and money. There were tensions between conservatives and Fascists, however, for Fascists were dismissive of the 'feminine' softness of the bourgeoisie. They announced the advent of a new manly elite, tempered by war, ready to do whatever was necessary to defeat the nation's enemies. Fascists also castigated the idleness of the bourgeoisie, and saw themselves as representatives of those who worked – those who were competent to govern the country and create a new Italy. Alarmingly, Fascists were as likely to fight conservative nationalists on the streets as to collaborate with them. Mussolini remained reluctant to cut all ties with the Socialists. And whereas the wealthy would have been content just to see Socialist and Catholic organizations destroyed, Fascists set about forming unions of their own. They drew upon a pre-existing fund of conservatism amongst some peasants and workers, while carrot-and-stick methods encouraged many more to join. However, the Fascists did not condemn private property itself, so they were, in the eyes of the wealthy, far better than the left. Conservatives were reassured when at the end of 1921 Fascism became an organized party, the *Partito Nazionale Fascista* (PNF), and embraced monarchism and liberal economics.

Fascism was still not a force in parliament – it won only 35 seats in the 1921 elections. It came to power through a combination of pressure from the streets and backing from the country's business, agrarian, and political elites. In the summer of 1922 grassroots Fascist pressure for the capture of power intensified, and in the autumn plans for a 'March on Rome' were laid. Liberal politicians faced a thorny choice. If they resisted, the army and police, which had proved rather ambivalent in their attitude, might refuse to fight the Fascists. Even if the Fascists were defeated, the left might profit. Politicians, business, and army agreed that it would be safest to bring the Fascists into the government. Doing so might stiffen the authorities' resolve against the left, and even revitalize the Italian body politic. Dangerously, the Liberals compensated for their loss of votes to Catholic and Socialist parties by using Fascism as an alternative source of mass support. Mussolini became prime minister on 29 October 1922.

Assured of the support of administration and army, Fascists attacked the left with impunity. In 1923 the Catholic *Popolari* disintegrated too under the dual impact of *squadristi* attacks and the removal of Papal support – Mussolini promised the Papacy improvement in the Church's position in return for this favour. Beyond this, it was far from certain what Fascism stood for. There were at least three possibilities. Now that the Party was in power, conservatives flooded into it, especially in the south (accompanied by Mafia bands). Conservatives hoped that Mussolini would re-establish law and order, and that 'normalization' would follow. They wanted a more authoritarian version of the old system, in which their own rights and monopoly on social and political power would be guaranteed, but they believed parliamentary government and a degree of political liberty to be essential to the maintenance of their influence. Members of the old Italian Nationalist Association, which had merged with the PNF in 1923, wanted a more authoritarian state, but were not enamoured of disorderly *squadristi*. Many Fascists, in contrast, called for a 'second

3. The March on Rome, 28 October 1922. From left to right, Italo Balbo, Mussolini, Cesare Maria De Vecchi and Emilio De Bono.

revolution' to displace established politicians. These radicals included syndicalist intellectuals and Fascist trade union leaders, feminists, local Party bosses hungry for power, and economic modernizers.

Mussolini did not side clearly with any tendency. He did, however, alter the electoral law in such a way as to win the Fascists a majority in parliament in 1924. During the election campaign the Fascists engaged in an orgy of violence against the Socialists, but went too far when they murdered the Socialist spokesman, Giacomo Matteotti. Mussolini was implicated in the crime and there was an outcry from the left and even from Liberals such as Giolitti and the conservative Salandra. Mussolini at first made concessions to the conservatives, but this only caused radicals to intensify their calls for a 'second revolution'. Fascist unions piled on the pressure against business, while Fascist women renewed demands for female suffrage.

In January 1925 Mussolini bowed to radical pressure and declared his intention to install a genuinely Fascist regime. Conservatives did not desert him because to have done so might have led to recovery of the left. At the end of the year political opposition was banned, freedom of the press ceased, and election of local governments ended.

Historians have concurred that the radicals' victory was empty, and that the regime was never truly fascistized. There is less agreement about the nature of the regime that did emerge. Some have argued that it was dominated by the heirs of the INA. The latter, remember, wanted a strong state to nationalize Italians and restore bourgeois society through discipline and hierarchy. Influenced by German philosophy, they held that individual freedom was meaningful only where a strong *state* expressed the national interest. The INA therefore opposed radical Fascists' demands for *party* supervision of the administration, army, and civil service. They insisted that Fascists obey the law rather than make it up themselves. In terms of the definitions presented in Chapter 2, the INA was situated somewhere between authoritarian conservatism and fascism.

The INA stalwarts Luigi Federzoni, as interior minister in 1926, and Alfredo Rocco, as minister of justice from 1925 to 1932, helped lay the foundations of the regime. Fascist violence was gradually ended. The state set up its own youth and women's organizations in an attempt to realize the INA's dream of the 'nation-mobilized-from-above'. Established interests meanwhile retained freedom of action. The monarchy remained in place, while big business and agrarians retained much influence. In 1929 Mussolini delivered on his promise to the Pope. The Lateran Pact ended six decades of papal opposition to the Italian state, and accorded the Church considerable rights in education and youth work.

The violent grassroots rural fascism epitomized by Roberto Farinacci was weakened. In contrast to the Nazis, radical Fascists largely failed to destroy the rule of law and de-structure the administration. By the late 1920s the prevailing image of the Fascist was no longer the young, single man who fought Socialists whilst professing not to 'give a damn', but the responsible husband and father who worked from nine to six in the building of a new nation, as his wife bore babies for Italy. During these years those who saw Fascism as a vehicle for the realization of feminist demands, or for autonomous trade unionism within a corporatist economy, were frustrated (see Chapters 9 and 10).

However, fascist radicals were never completely marginalized, and the regime didn't become just another of the royal-bureaucratic dictatorships so common in inter-war Europe (see Chapter 6). Mussolini never wanted such a regime, and so he was obliged to use the Party as a lever against conservatives. The Party remained an independent body, and few of its leaders possessed, or were allowed to possess, additional posts in state service. The Party never abandoned its desire for control over welfare, education, and leisure – for the mobilized nation.

Farinacci's role as general secretary was crucial. His backing for a centralized dictatorship inadvertently reduced the freedom of action of local Fascist radicals, and in 1926 random Fascist violence ceased. Yet radicalism now took a different form. Farinacci tried to use the Party to bypass normal bureaucratic methods of government and create a new governing class. Farinacci was soon ousted, but his successors, Augusto Turati and Achille Starace, pursued the same goals more circumspectly. The Party became an inflated parallel bureaucracy, and a Party card became a prerequisite of advancement in state service. Often civil servants merely paid lip service to Fascist ideals, but the essential point is that ideological conformity mattered as much as normal methods of selecting and training bureaucrats in the Fascist state. In 1932 Mussolini demanded that graduates of the Fascist Academy of Political Sciences (created in 1928) be given access to state jobs. Ultranationalist ideology rather than rules would become the basis of administration.

In effect, there was something of a stand-off. The Party, along with big business, the Church, state, army, Fascist unions, and corporations became one of several semi-autonomous power centres in Fascist Italy. There was much rivalry and confusion between them. For instance, the Fascist workers' leisure organization, Dopolavoro, began as a state organization, but was taken over by the Party in 1927 in an attempt to undermine the influence of Fascist unions over workers. Dopolavoro still had to compete with Catholic organizations and Fascist trade unions for workers' loyalties, however. The history of women's and youth organizations was marked by similar conflicts.

The Duce wanted the final say in all disputes. He pored over state papers in his study until the small hours. At one time he nominally headed eight ministries. Obviously he couldn't really decide everything. His interventions were haphazard, ill prepared, and there was plenty of room for others to take initiatives. Mussolini was nevertheless essential to the functioning of the regime. His power, when he chose to exercise it, was immense. He was considerably more popular than any of his deputies, and so none of the latter could easily risk going against his express will. This was especially true in foreign affairs, the one area Mussolini clearly chose to make his own. In the 1930s the drive to war inaugurated a new radicalization of the regime.

Mussolini's foreign adventurism was the fruit of three factors. Firstly, Fascists had always seen the conquest of new territory as the best means to resolve economic problems, and regarded war as intrinsically good for the nation. Secondly, fascistization of the Foreign Ministry reduced conservative opposition to his adventurism. Although Mussolini's foreign policy had precedents in the pre-Fascist epoch, it was marked by Fascist ideology. Expansion was justified by the Darwinian struggle between nations, and by the need for Italy to find living space for surplus population. Thirdly, the rise of Hitler made it possible for Italy, insufficiently strong on its own, to revise the Versailles Treaty. At first Mussolini was wary of German expansionism, for Italy included German-speaking minorities which it was feared might come into Hitler's sights should he succeed in annexing Austria to the Reich. Soon, however, it became clear that German military strength on the Continent was so great that the only way to expand Italian power was in alliance with Hitler and at the expense of British and French interests in the Mediterranean and Africa. Italian armies invaded Abyssinia in 1935, fought on the side of Franco's right-wing alliance in the Spanish Civil War in 1936–9, and occupied Albania in 1939. In the following year Italy participated in the invasion of France (just before the French surrender to Germany), and in 1941 invaded Greece and began an advance on Egypt.

Gearing up the nation for war, together with economic crisis, radicalized the regime and altered the balance between its components in favour of Party organizations and new state agencies. The regime redoubled its efforts to achieve economic self-sufficiency, which implied greater regulation of the economy and intervention in private life. The population was encouraged to eat home-grown rice rather than imported pasta – a nation of spaghetti eaters, Mussolini once declared, could never restore Roman civilization. During the depression, moreover, the government created a state holding company, the *Istituto per la ricostruzione Industriale* (IRI), which established *de facto* control over failing firms. In 1936 the large banks were nationalized. These measures did not threaten the existence of big business *per se*. In fact very large concerns gained at the expense of smaller competitors. But business was enmeshed in state controls – precisely the sort of thing it had hoped to avoid by helping the Fascists into power.

War also meant further mobilization of the population. Under Achille Starace, secretary from 1931 to 1939, the Party 'went to the masses', enrolling huge numbers of women and students in Party groups (the last vestiges of an autonomous feminist movement were eradicated). Starace organized ritual adoration of Mussolini in mass demonstrations, and took special interest in the regulation of workers' leisure in the Dopolavoro. In 1938 nationalism became out and out racism, first in Abyssinia, then in Italy itself, where antisemitic laws were introduced in 1938.

The totalitarian intention behind these measures is evident, but in practice little was achieved. They were implemented in a confused manner, and in any case Italy may not have had the infrastructure and resources required for genuine regulation of social life. Worse, from the regime's point of view, 'going to the people' alarmed the fiefdoms within the regime – business, Church, and monarch. Signs of popular discontent appeared. A gap between the regime's propaganda image and its practical achievements was becoming obvious to some intellectuals.

The Italian war effort was unimpressive. The masses had no desire to fight. German assistance was required to rescue Mussolini's forces in Greece and North Africa. In 1943 the Allies invaded Italy, and the Fascist Grand Council and King conspired to evict

Mussolini from office. Italy became a battlefield, with Germany occupying the north and the Allies the south. The Duce was imprisoned, but was soon rescued by German forces. Until the end of the war he headed the German puppet Salò Republic, in which Fascist die-hards attempted to implement Fascism in its 'pure' form, whilst engaged in armed struggle with a mass resistance movement.

Chapter 5
Germany: the racial state

There are sufficient similarities between Fascism and Nazism to make it worthwhile applying the concept of fascism to both. In Italy and Germany a movement came to power that sought to create national unity through the repression of national enemies and the incorporation of all classes and both genders into a permanently mobilized nation. This was a totalitarian project, if impossible to realize.

One reason for the ultimate failure of totalitarianism in Italy and Germany was that the ideal national community was envisaged in such a way that it required the elites to give up far less than the left. In Italy, the Catholic Church, monarchy, and a tradition of liberal humanism within the elites constituted significant barriers to totalitarianism. In Germany, the army had been reduced in size by the Versailles Treaty, Catholicism was weaker, Protestant churches were traditionally favourable to authority, and conservative parties had already imbibed many of the ideas of the radical right before 1914. Nevertheless, non-fascist conservatism was never completely eliminated from the Nazi regime.

In both countries there was permanent rivalry between the fascist party and its offshoots on the one hand, and established institutions on the other, within limits set by personal loyalty to Mussolini and Hitler. Established institutions were soon on the back foot in both

4. Hitler and Mussolini caught by the camera at the Tomb of Fascist Martyrs, Florence, 10 October 1938.

countries, especially in Germany, where Himmler managed, with Hitler's approval, to fuse the SS (*Schutzstaffel*, or special security forces) and the police, thereby realizing one of the conditions for the extermination of the Jews. Each side in this deadly rivalry attempted to appeal to the leader against their rivals, thereby enhancing Mussolini's and Hitler's popularity – already immense because of their perceived success in re-establishing their respective countries as world powers.

From the mid-1920s Hitler regarded himself as the great leader possessed of messianic vision who would lead Germany to victory or death. Germany's mission, he believed, was the conquest of living space in the East, at the expense of 'Judeo-Bolshevik' Russia. Germany's ability to achieve this goal depended on overcoming its own decadence by breaking with democracy and purging itself of racial enemies. Living space would in turn provide the resources needed to unite the people in a racially pure Germany. Domestic and foreign policy objectives were mutually dependent.

In themselves these ideas were crude. They were powerful because they issued from the Wagnerian strand in German culture, and derived from 19th-century social Darwinist, imperialist, and racist ideas which had been dressed up as 'science' in certain university faculties and professions, where they informed a host of projects for the engineering of a strong society. Hitler's fixations, including his Jewish obsessions, were not shared by the whole German population, or even by all Nazis. But Hitler's huge popularity permitted him to implement his radical racial and military schemes. He was certain, too, of the backing of the Nazi hierarchy, linked to him by personal loyalty.

How could such a movement have come to power? The correlation between the gravity of social crisis and the triumph of fascism was not straightforward, for although the upheaval that followed the Great War was at least as serious in Germany as in Italy, fascism did not immediately profit. Defeat in 1918 led to the collapse of the authoritarian monarchical regime. Workers' and soldiers' councils were set up, and a Soviet republic briefly ruled Bavaria. The new Weimar Republic made major concessions to trade unions and granted women the vote, and socialism made massive gains in the elections of 1919.

Nationalists were stunned by the harshness of the peace treaty of 1919, which amputated much German territory. They blamed democrats and socialists for having 'stabbed Germany in the back' in 1918. As in Italy a right-wing reaction developed, consisting of an alliance of mainstream conservatives, Pan-Germans, demobilized soldiers' groups such as the Freikorps, and new paramilitary nationalist movements including Hitler's National Socialists. Radical ultranationalism had resurfaced in the crisis. In 1920 the Pan-German Kapp attempted a coup in Berlin, and in 1923 Hitler, in alliance with General Ludendorff, tried another in Munich – the 'Beer Hall Putsch'.

For the moment, however, the Weimar Republic survived. Unlike their Italian counterparts, German socialists defended the regime against the right, and a general strike ensured Kapp's failure. The army knew anyway that Britain and France would not tolerate a nationalist regime in Germany, so it too accepted democracy for the moment. By 1933, many of those who had defended Weimar at its inception had joined the ranks of its irreducible opponents.

During the 1920s the Weimar Republic appeared to achieve a degree of stability. The economic situation improved, to some extent. Centrist coalitions managed, just about, to impose stable government. Rapprochement with France and Britain held out some hope that Germany might recover its eastern territories. Political violence almost subsided. Yet the Republic remained fragile. On the left the Communist Party (KPD) never accepted the 'bourgeois republic', while on the right the Nationalist DNVP remained monarchist. The paramilitary veterans' association, the

Stahlhelm, was strongly entrenched in Protestant, bourgeois provincial society, and nourished hostility both to the Social Democrats and Communists and to the established right. Those who would vote Nazi in the 1930s had already espoused populist ultranationalist politics in the previous decade and perhaps before 1914, and had voted for a host of nationalist splinter parties in the 1920s. These voters condemned the subservience of the Weimar system to selfish economic interests and demanded a more 'national' policy while paradoxically seeking more effective defence of their own special interests. Weimar politics degenerated into a free-for-all in which each interest group accused rival interest groups of refusing to put the national interest first. The Nazis triumphed because they managed to convince wide sections of the electorate that they could reconcile sectional interests with the nation.

The American economic crash in 1929 had a grave impact on Germany's fragile society. The Slump led to business collapses, indebtedness for farmers, and massive unemployment. The Republic lost whatever legitimacy it had possessed, as conservatives felt unable to tolerate its perceived favouritism towards workers, feminists, and Jews. Many of the six million unemployed abandoned a regime that seemed to have brought misery. Communists and Nazis both gained votes. Parliamentary government was impossible, and from 1930 governments had to rule by decree. The army, no longer so fearful of the Allies, intervened regularly in politics. German democracy was moribund well before Hitler seized power.

In prison for his part in the 1923 putsch, Hitler became convinced that the party could win power only through the ballot box. Electoral propaganda was at first primarily directed at industrial workers, in the hope of detaching them from the KPD. But the 1928 elections showed unexpected gains amongst the Protestant peasantry, who had suffered badly from the agricultural crisis. From then on Nazi propaganda was targeted at conservative voters, and the Nazis won most of their votes from this source. Although the left posed less of a threat at this time than it had just after the war, the Nazis engaged in a campaign of intimidation against Socialists, Communists, and Catholics, thereby presenting themselves as the only force able to restore order. They simultaneously adopted an anti-establishment stance, portraying themselves as the real representatives of the people, and denouncing successive conservative governments as unrepresentative.

Although this populist message was particularly attractive to ex-conservatives, the Nazi vote was broader than that of other parties. The movement won a significant minority of votes from the left. It appealed more or less equally to men and women. Around a quarter of the German working class, especially workers in small concerns in small towns, may have voted Nazi in July 1932.

Despite the relative breadth of their appeal, the Nazis, with 37% of the vote in July 1932, didn't have enough seats in parliament to govern. In a new election in November they lost two million votes. So how did Hitler win power? As in Italy, he did so through a combination of alliance with conservatives and pressure from the streets. Conservative politicians, like the business, military, and land-owning elites, were certainly hostile to the Republic, yet they distrusted the Nazis as 'brown Bolsheviks', and preferred an authoritarian government run by themselves. The problem was that the elites, rightly or wrongly, felt that no government could survive without mass support. This conviction testified to the extent to which 'democratic' assumptions had penetrated even the reactionary right. It also reflected army fears that it wouldn't be able to maintain order if both Communists and Nazis remained hostile to the regime. General Schleicher tried to resolve this problem by offering trade union leaders and radical Nazis an innovative programme of economic recovery, but this was not at all what most conservatives wanted. For want of alternatives, the conservatives made Hitler chancellor on 30 January 1933.

Besides Hitler, the Nazis only had two posts in the cabinet. But control over the police, coupled with the right to govern by decree, permitted them to unleash a wave of repression against the left. The burning down of the Reichstag on 27 February served as a pretext to suspend freedom of the press and association. In the elections of 5 March the Nazis did not do quite as well as expected, but they did obtain a majority with their DNVP allies. The Enabling Act, passed by the Reichstag on 23 March, formed the basis of dictatorship. In subsequent weeks trade unions were banned, and non-Nazi right-wing parties dissolved themselves. One of the first acts of the regime was to remove Jews from state employment.

Meanwhile, conservatives and radicals jostled for power within the regime. The Nazis' strong-arm wing, the SA (*Sturmabteilung*), which had led the campaign against the left, demanded a second revolution. The army feared that the SA wished to usurp its position. Partly because of conservative pressure, Hitler arrested and executed the SA's leadership on 30 June 1934 – the 'night of the long knives'. But this did not permit conservatives to regain lost ground, for the repression was not carried out by the state or army, but by another wing of the Nazi movement – the SS. A few weeks later the army swore an oath of loyalty to Hitler.

Nazi radicalism was evident especially in the political sphere. The destruction of the rule of law meant not only arbitrary beatings, imprisonment in concentration camps, or execution, but the erosion of the very basis of rule-based government, justice, and administration. The civil service was purged, and the institutions of the Party and SS became a sort of parallel administration, the personnel of which was recruited on the basis of ideology and service to the Party, rather than the established procedures of the civil service. Many people of unorthodox background rose into positions of influence. This was not revolution as Marxists would recognize it, but it represented destabilization of existing power structures.

As with Fascism in Italy, trade union radicals and those who hoped that Nazism would render women more equal were largely disappointed by Nazism in power (see Chapters 9 and 10). Yet the Nazis were more successful in ensuring that their dogma penetrated into all spheres of society. School syllabuses were reformed; all independent associations, from women's groups to film societies, were dissolved or incorporated into Nazi organizations. The German Labour Front, a manifestation of the Nazis' corporatist schemes and the workers' leisure organization, the sinisterly named Strength Through Joy, were both heavily involved in the engineering of the Nazi Utopia.

The guiding principle in all of this was race. Although antisemitism was not shared by all Germans, and although biological antisemitism was not widespread, the collapse of the Weimar Republic had permitted a movement to seize power in which biological racism emphatically was an article of faith, especially amongst the leadership. Hitler's enormous popularity, earned by crushing Communism and restoring Germany's international position, coupled with indifference to the fate of the Jews in many quarters and internalization to some extent of the regime's propaganda, provided antisemites with the leverage necessary to implement their designs. More will be said on this topic in subsequent chapters. For the moment suffice it to say that racial considerations suffused all aspects of policy, from the protection of mothers and the distribution of medical care to diplomacy and educational syllabuses.

Nazi racial policies could not have been implemented without the assistance of non-Nazi institutions, especially the army, civil service, and academics. The uneven impact of Nazi radicalism meant that as in Italy big business, the army, and certain ministries retained some independence, and there was much competition between them and the agencies of party and state. Yet the balance of power was different to that in Italy. Business lost its ability to influence government policy collectively, as it became increasingly subject to regulation. In 1938 many generals were dismissed and Hitler became commander-in-chief. The SS, under Heinrich Himmler, established its own military force and extended its reach into all areas of racial policy – since racial policy was fundamental to Nazism the arbitrary power of the SS was enormous.

Since the German army, civil service, and professoriate were more open to the fascist message than their Italian counterparts, the various components of the regime outdid each other in their endeavours to realize the Führer's broad agenda – they worked, as Ian Kershaw has argued, 'towards the Führer'. There was no need for Hitler to dictate detailed policy – in any case he had neither the energy nor the aptitude to intervene systematically in domestic affairs. This does not mean that the regime did not aspire to totalitarianism. The confusion of powers liberated policy-makers from the constraints of morality and law. It made uncertainty a principle of government and reduced the regime's victims to helplessness.

Like Mussolini, Hitler was passionately interested in diplomacy. He had always regarded the acquisition of *lebensraum* and the elimination of race enemies and Bolshevism as essential to the establishment of a harmonious German society. Hitler did not have a clear idea of how he would achieve these aims, but he did set about preparing Germany for racial war. Most domestic policy was related in one way or another to this priority. Measures to encourage women to marry and bear children were intended to increase the size of the 'healthy' population and provide future soldiers. Sterilization of the 'unfit' would improve the quality of the population. Public works projects had a military dimension; the Four Year Plan of 1936 emphasized arms production and import substitution. It was no accident that the radicalization of Jewish policy in November 1938 followed a war scare. Removal of Jewish influence – extermination was not yet Nazi policy – was seen by the Nazis both as the goal of war and the precondition of success.

Hitler's diplomacy was not guided by a clear medium-term plan. His hope that Britain might remain neutral and leave Germany free to dominate the Continent was soon disappointed. In 1936, however, Hitler told his generals that a war for living space must take place by 1940 at the latest, and in the following year he seized whatever opportunity came his way. He annexed Austria to the Reich in March 1938, and turned his attention to the Sudeten German minority in Czechoslovakia in September. War finally broke out with Britain and France in September 1939 when Hitler, reassured by alliance with the Soviet Union, invaded Poland. Almost as soon as France had been defeated in 1940, Hitler began to plan an invasion of the Soviet Union.

Hitler's invasion of the Soviet Union unleashed a conflict of unprecedented barbarity. The total destruction of indigenous authority in the conquered eastern lands, and the absence of the constraints represented by the bureaucracy within Germany, permitted Nazi organizations to kill, torture, exploit, plunder, and experiment upon defeated populations in line with Hitler's apocalyptic prophesies. Even before war began, Hitler had declared that war would end with the annihilation of European Jewry, and so it turned out.

Hitler's fantastic delusions survived the complete collapse of German armies. In his Berlin bunker, he and Goebbels looked to tarot cards and Frederick the Great for inspiration. His last testament blamed the German people for having failed him.

Chapter 6
Fascisms and conservatisms in the early 20th century

Imitations of Italian and German fascism appeared all over Europe and the Americas in the inter-war years. Close inspection reveals that some were not actually very similar to their supposed models. Foreign imitators interpreted fascism according to their own lights. They borrowed some features, modified others, and did not see some important aspects at all. So not everyone who called themselves a fascist was one in the sense in which we are interested. The Mexican Goldshirts, organized in 1934, mimicked Italian and German styles, but their nationalism was really closer to that of the pre-1914 European radical right. Much the same applied to ultranationalist groups in 1930s Japan. They admired some aspects of Nazism, demanded institutional reform, militarization, and expansion overseas, but they would have regarded the organization of a popular nationalist movement as a crime against the emperor.

Genuine fascist movements also emerged – even in countries with strong democratic traditions. In the United States, the American-German Bund was genuinely fascist, but gained at most 6,000 members at its peak.

The movement was partly a product of the ill treatment of Germans, which had been common since America entered the

5. A mass rally of the German-American Volksbund at Madison Square Garden, New York, in February 1939. Note the swastikas superimposed upon the American eagle.

Great War (this was the period when the frankfurter was renamed the hot dog). Although the Bund established some links with the KKK, its appeal was restricted by this same anti-Germanism. Father Charles E. Coughlin's National Union For Social Justice, founded in 1934, was larger but less extreme – Coughlin won a million votes in the 1934 presidential elections. The British Union of Fascists (BUF), founded in 1932 by the former Labour Party minister Sir Oswald Mosley, was another movement modelled explicitly on fascist movements, and which meets the criteria laid out in Chapter 2. The movement only flourished briefly under the patronage of the *Daily Mail*, but soon declined. That Mosley's sister-in-law, Nancy Mitford, henceforth referred to him as 'the poor old leader' adequately sums up Mosley's subsequent status as a voice crying in the wilderness.

The Croix de feu in France rejected the fascist label, and its leader, Colonel de La Rocque, was a rather dilatory man. He nevertheless led a mass paramilitary movement that threatened 'defensive' violence in the hope of persuading established politicians that it alone could govern France effectively. The Croix de feu saw itself as the embodiment of the people and the vehicle of a veteran elite which would regenerate France, following the sweeping away of communism and established conservatism. The movement aspired to capture the leadership of the working class from the left, and integrate labour into a corporatist system. It was extremely antifeminist, and yet mobilized women in a huge politicized welfare organization, which refused aid to the millions of poor immigrant workers in France.

Fascists in the United States, Britain, and France didn't come close to power. It is perhaps surprising that fascism should have been so weak in the United States, given the extent of racism in mainstream Protestant opinion (the KKK may have had between two and eight million members in the early 1920s), the severity of the economic crisis, conservative dislike of President Roosevelt's New Deal, and the extent of isolationist opposition to American involvement in the struggle against fascism in Europe. The most convincing explanation for the failure of fascism is that the social policies of the New Deal channelled anti-establishment populism into the left rather than the extreme right. This was all the more possible because racism was not absent from the mainstream left or right in America.

Britain was not free from tension either. Although the country was on the winning side in the Great War, the Empire was threatened by insurgent nationalism, while the General Strike of 1926 and the rise of the Labour Party was seen by many as a danger to property. Nevertheless, the BUF found that established conservatives were more united than their German or Italian counterparts and were so well entrenched in parliament that they had no need of fascist backing. Some, perhaps complacently, see Britain's long tradition of representative government as a barrier to fascism. The fact that the country's electoral system makes it difficult to vote for extremist parties without letting in one's political opponents might be more important than any uniquely British fund of wisdom and tolerance.

In France, the position was somewhat more favourable to fascists, for many conservatives were critical of parliamentarianism, and fear of communism was enormous. Yet, the French left learned the lessons of Germany, where socialists and communists had hated each other almost as much as they did the Nazis. The French left united against fascism, and proved adept at fighting it in the streets. It targeted its policies at those electors they considered most vulnerable to fascism, winning a large majority in the elections of 1936. The strength of antifascism convinced many conservatives that support for fascism was risky. The Croix de feu submitted tamely to dissolution in June 1936. It reappeared as the Parti social français (PSF), which slowly shook off its more fascistic characteristics, only to rediscover its antipathy to democracy when France was occupied by the Germans in 1940.

Fascists rarely won power through their own efforts, and rarely dominated governments. In the many cases in which democracies fell 'to the right', conservative dictatorships profited. This happened most often in Eastern and southern Europe, and in Latin America. In Europe, significant fascist movements emerged and challenged conservative dictatorships; in Latin America, this was rare.

Before we proceed, it is worth reminding ourselves of our definition of fascism so that we can use it (that's what definitions are for) to make sense of political developments in the states under consideration. The essential point is that authoritarian conservatism governs through the Church, civil service, army, and perhaps a monarchy. Authoritarian conservatism defends family and property tenaciously, and insofar as it is interested in mass mobilization, it organizes it under the leadership of the established authorities. Fascism, in contrast, endeavours to bring a new elite to power as representative of the mobilized people, and regards defence of property and family as subordinate to the needs of the mobilized nation.

Conservatives and fascists, nevertheless, share enemies, and so collaboration is always possible. Indeed, as Martin Blinkhorn has argued, in inter-war Europe there was a continuum from authoritarian conservatism to fascism. At one end were authoritarian conservative regimes possessed of minimal fascist tendencies, such as the Salazar dictatorship in Portugal. At the other end were fascist movements and regimes with minimal conservative involvement, of which Nazism is the best example. Even the latter, and still more Italian Fascism, were not pure examples of fascism. The situation is further complicated by ongoing disputes within fascist movements about whether to emphasize the radical or the reactionary sides of fascism. And in conservative parties, there were often elements that wanted to pep up traditional conservatism through selective borrowings from fascism. The precise nature of fascism, its relationship with conservative forces, and its chances of winning power therefore varied enormously from country to country.

Clerical fascism?

The Spanish dictatorship of General Francisco Franco is sometimes seen as fascist. In July 1936 Franco led a military rising against the Spanish republic, and by the end of the ensuing Civil War he had established a dictatorship which lasted until his death in 1975. The coalition supporting Franco included a fascist component, the Falange Española, under José Antonio Primo de Rivera. In the familiar manner, the Falange expanded rapidly at the expense of constitutional Catholic conservatism, as the latter was thrown out of government in 1935 and then defeated by the left in a general election in February 1936. The Falange showed all the classic features of fascism. Of particular interest was its commitment to a form of corporatism – 'national syndicalism' – meant to be freer of business and state control than Italian and German versions, and its demand for land reform and nationalization of banks and credit. The Falange was more religious than most fascist movements, without, however, placing Catholic universalism above the nation. The Falange played an important part in crushing the left within areas controlled by the Francoists.

The Falange was typical of fascist movements in that radicals and conservatives struggled for power within it. Circumstances in Spain ensured that authoritarian conservatives largely won out. Before the 1930s politicization was limited in poverty-stricken Spain. The collapse of constitutional conservatism in 1935 led to an influx of conservatives and even monarchists into the Falange, many of whom were not fascists at all. Spain also lacked a strong ultranationalist tradition, not least because it was a multiethnic state (comprising Castillians, Catalans, and Basques). Neither had Spain experienced the upheaval of the Great War. For all these reasons the Falange was unable to use a mass party to win power, and lacking this leverage it gained little autonomy. Within Franco's coalition, the Falange had to compete with the Catholic and conservative Carlists, and with monarchists. The latter were strengthened by family and class links with the officer corps, which distrusted Falangist radicalism. While the army was rendered indispensable by the stubbornness of Republican military defence, many Falangist activists were killed or imprisoned by the Republicans.

The Falangists did not resist when in 1937 Franco united the Carlists, monarchists, and Falange in a single movement. Franco's regime was not dissimilar to Mussolini's in that there was a single party that included hard-line fascists as well as conservatives. The fascist component was weaker in Spain, however, and contrary to what happened in Italy and Germany, the Church, army, and administration became stronger with time.

The Catholic-military-bureaucratic Francoist dictatorship's closest cousin in inter-war Europe was the Austrian Ständestaat (corporatist state) of 1933–8 under Engelbert Dollfuss and then Kurt von Schuschnigg. In Austria, too, there was a subordinate fascistic element in the shape of the 'Austro-fascist' Heimwehr, but it acted more as an ally of the government than as an alternative power source. The most important distinguishing feature of the Heimwehr was that it was torn between affinity with Nazi Germany and a desire to revive the supranational Austro-Hungarian Empire in the form of a pro-Italian, Austria-led confederation of Catholic states. Catholicism was to be the basis of an Austrian national identity capable of undermining the attraction of union with largely Protestant Germany. This supranationalism somewhat diluted the Heimwehr's fascism. The Heimwehr was, nevertheless, too radical and too antisemitic for the leaders of the Ständestaat, and in 1936 the government dissolved it. In 1938 Hitler, with the support of the Austro-Nazis, overthrew the Ständestaat on the grounds that it was a 'reactionary' regime – there was some truth in this.

6. Fascism and authoritarian conservatism: From left to right Engelbert Dollfuss of Austria, Mussolini and Major Gyula Gömbös the semifascist Prime Minister of Hungary in Rome, 17 March 1934. On the right is a representative of the Japanese dictatorship.

Eastern Europe

The new democracies of Eastern Europe, which had been created in a wave of optimism out of the ruins of the multinational Russian, German, and Austro-Hungarian empires, toppled like ninepins during the inter-war years. Czechoslovakia alone avoided a *coup d'état*, only to fall into the Nazis' clutches in 1938–9.

The apprentice democracies suffered all of the problems of Italy and Germany – wartime destruction, popular unrest, strikes, economic difficulties, and ethnic tensions. We find the same pervasive fear of Bolshevism, exacerbated in some cases by actual war with the Bolsheviks. The Soviet Union had territorial claims on many Eastern European states, and there was a rash of communist insurrections. Communists attempted to exploit the grievances not only of the working classes, but of peasants (who wanted more land), and of ethnic minorities. We find in Eastern Europe the same conviction that the war had upset the normal balance between the sexes. As in Italy and Germany, conservatives called for tougher measures against communists, feminists, and ethnic minorities in the name of national unity.

This was a powerful message in the ethnic maelstrom of inter-war Eastern Europe. The peace treaties had supposedly been based on national self-determination. But entanglement of ethnic groups was so complex that it was impossible to make international frontiers coincide with them. The new 'national' states all included substantial ethnic minorities – Poland, for instance, was only 70% Polish. Formerly subject nationalities became masters of new minorities. Often, victorious nationalists broke with the left-wing heritage of nationalism (in any case sometimes superficial) and became intolerant, anticommunist, and antifeminist.

At first, there were signs that the various ethnic groups were prepared to live and let live, for peace treaties required protection of minority rights. Soon, however, border disputes developed, and some frontiers were settled by force. Moreover, Germany, Bulgaria, Austria, and Hungary resented having lost territory and were sensitive to the fortunes of fellow nationals who had been reduced to the status of minorities in other states – Hungarians in Romania, or Germans in Poland. Those states that had gained through expansion (Romania and Serbia – which became Yugoslavia) or that had been newly created (Estonia, Latvia, Lithuania, Czechoslovakia) wanted to 'nationalize' or exclude minorities. In Eastern Europe, as in the west, democracy often meant dictatorship of the majority, not toleration or still less multiculturalism.

The intolerant tendencies within democracy did not assuage those who were convinced that democracy accorded too much freedom to ethnic minorities, workers, and women. In state after state, conservatives installed authoritarian regimes which repudiated treaty obligations to protect minorities, arrested communists, and declared their intention to return women to the home. The left often identified these regimes with fascism. In fact they ruled through established institutions. The churches gained much influence: in Romania Orthodox primate Miron Cristea became prime minister in 1938. The army became the mainstay of government in Poland. Landed magnates remained preponderant in Hungary. In Bulgaria, Romania, and Yugoslavia monarchies governed directly. Everywhere civil servants were influential.

Elitist as they were, some of these dictatorships created organizations designed to provide them with mass support. In 1935 the Polish 'colonels' set up the Camp of National Unity. Similarly, the Yugoslav Radical Union was designed to provide popular support for a royal dictatorship – members even wore green shirts. The Yugoslav regime also accepted support from the Yugoslav Women's Union, seeing its educational and welfare activities as a means to encourage loyalty to the monarchy. None of these organizations resembled fascist mass parties. They deferred to the established authorities, and they had no organizational monopoly. Indeed, one of the distinguishing marks of these dictatorships was that they tolerated a degree of political freedom. Censorship was not complete; the opposition was subject to arrest and imprisonment, but continued to exist. Constitutions were modified, ballots were manipulated, but elections were still held. In general, the law was still observed, albeit a markedly authoritarian law.

This is precisely why fascists opposed these dictatorships. We must be cautious, however, for significant fascist movements did not emerge in all those countries in which circumstances were apparently favourable. In Czechoslovakia and Yugoslavia fascist movements might have been expected to emerge amongst Czech or Serb nationalities. Both might have seen their governments as too attentive to ethnic minorities, and both countries experienced economic problems and left-wing agitation. In Czechoslovakia, however, there was simply no political space for fascism, for the working class was monopolized by socialism, and the government had been remarkably successful in appeasing the discontent of farmers through a programme of price support. What is more, whilst Czech nationalism possessed its blind spots, Czechs prided themselves on being more tolerant and enlightened than Germans. Indeed, it was amongst the German minority in the Sudetenland region that fascism developed, thanks to the growth of opinion favouring union with Germany.

In Yugoslavia some small fascist movements did emerge, but there was no basis for extreme nationalism, for there was little Yugoslav patriotism. Although the dominant Serbs felt that the government made too many concessions to Croats and Slovene minorities, it was unrealistic to push for Serbianization of the country, given that Serbs themselves were a minority. In any case, Yugoslavia was a poor country, which might not have possessed the level of development needed for the organization of mass political parties.

Eastern European fascism was most successful in Hungary and Romania, and we shall use the latter as an example. One of the major issues in Romanian politics (as we saw in Chapter 1) was how to incorporate the large ethnic minority populations acquired after the Great War into a Romanian national state. Nationalists were also fearful of communism – they believed that all communists were Jews and all Jews were communists. Another problem was that peasants, the overwhelming majority of the population, wanted more land.

As early as May 1920 a royal *coup d'état* prevented a peasant government from taking office. For eight years Romania was ruled by authoritarian 'liberal' governments. These administrations discriminated against non-Romanians in the economy and education and pursued a policy of economic modernization financed by high taxes on the peasantry. In 1928 the resulting peasant discontent permitted the National Peasant Party (NPP) to win office with a mandate to restore constitutional government and give land to the peasantry. In fact the NPP achieved little. Now that both parties had failed, power slipped back into the hands of the monarchy, while Codreanu's Legion of the Archangel Michael (the Iron Guard) provided the main opposition to the royal regime.

Romanian fascism developed from two sources. Firstly, the Legion won the support of peasants who had been disappointed by the record of the NPP – in any case the NPP had contained a strong fascistic element. Secondly, it recruited from disenchanted intellectuals, typified by Codreanu, who wanted to Romanianize the professions.

The Legion displayed all the characteristics of fascism. It claimed to issue from the people, depicting the peasantry as the essence of Romania. These views possessed the dual advantage of flattering the peasantry and legitimizing the claim of 'real' Romanians upon the professions. Unlike the Nazis, or even the Fascists, the Legion was strongly religious in tone, and was backed by many Orthodox priests. Codreanu saw the Romanian Orthodox religion as coterminous with Romanian nationality, so Jews were excluded from the nation both as an urban people and on religious grounds.

The Legion's religion was that, however, of a heretical sect. It was closely coupled to the romantic nationalist myth of Romanian rebirth long popular in intellectual circles, and was displayed through bizarre rituals which had little to do with organized religion (except as a form of grotesque mimicry – members of the Legion's death squads ritually drank each other's blood). Codreanu rejected the notion that religious principles should govern political behaviour. Politics was a domain of struggle and war, and the Legion was an extremely violent organization – Members' willingness to fight to the death was matched only in the SS, in which occult ideas were also present.

The Legion's belief that the nation was to be embodied in the people rather than in the dynasty did not render it popular with the church hierarchy or the monarchy. The government soon began to treat the Legion as an enemy on account of its radicalism. In 1937 the Legion gained 16% of the vote in a general election, while its ally the NPP also did well. In response, the king formed a frankly dictatorial government under Orthodox patriarch Miron Cristea. In 1938 the Legion was banned, and Codreanu was killed.

The Legion re-emerged in 1940, for the defeat of France destroyed the morale of the traditionally Francophile conservatives. Also in 1940 Hitler awarded large tracts of Romanian territory to Hungary and Bulgaria (Stalin helped himself to Bessarabia). The King was blamed for the destruction of the nation, and the Legion was vindicated. Under the conservative General Antonescu, the Legion was incorporated into government. This did not end the struggle between the old and new rights. Antonescu – typically of authoritarian conservatives – believed the Legion's confiscation of the businesses, farms, and homes of Jews and other minorities went too far. In January 1941 Antonescu won a trial of strength because the Nazis saw him as a more reliable ally than the ultranationalist Legion.

The failure of fascism to win power in Romania throws some light on the fortunes of fascism in other Eastern European states – especially in Hungary, Latvia, and Poland, where it was strongest. It is usually stated that fascist movements failed to win power in Eastern Europe because the threat from the left was insufficient to force conservatives to accept fascists as allies. This needs to be qualified, however, because although communist parties were weak, *fear* of communism was nourished by the Soviet Union's territorial ambitions and popular association of the Jews with communism. Moreover, it was generally believed that communism operated through secrecy and conspiracy, not through mass parties. So the very invisibility of communist parties increased fear of communism. In other words, we must examine beliefs prevailing at the time, rather than attribute views to historical actors based on our own perception of the level of the communist threat. To return to the point, there was, in principle, sufficient fear of communism to have brought fascists and conservatives together, and shared anticommunism often provided a basis for common action.

Why then did no more permanent alliance of fascists and conservatives come about? In Germany and Italy the long existence of parliament and the frequent practice of elections, although much disliked by conservatives, seems to have convinced them, probably wrongly, that governments must have some form of popular endorsement. Hence their reluctant quest for fascist support. In Eastern Europe, in contrast, conservatives were quite happy to suspend parliament whenever it looked as if fascism might become essential to the formation of a majority.

Another obstacle to cooperation was that Eastern European fascism was more socially radical than in Germany or Italy. Demands for the expropriation of Jewish property, and strikes against 'foreign' employers, looked very different in Eastern Europe, where Jews and other ethnic minorities made up a very large proportion of the bourgeoisie. What is more, fascists directly attacked the landowning indigenous elites by supporting peasant demands for land. Antonescu and his like saw little point in allying with movements that had almost as little regard for property as the communists.

Lacking conservative support, and unable to win elections, Eastern European fascists could win power only with support from the Nazis. Because the latter distrusted the fascists' extreme nationalism, this was not always forthcoming.

Latin America

Recourse to dictatorship was frequent in Latin America, and some regimes admired fascism and copied some of its features. Yet they never adopted all of them, and actually resembled the Italian Nationalist Association more than Mussolini's movement. Fascism rarely flourished in Latin America because levels of political mobilization in the poor societies of Latin America were very low. Neither had Latin America experienced anything like the Great War and its consequent brutalization and militarization of politics. Latin American governments, moreover, could with army backing easily suppress any kind of popular opposition, fascist included. In any case, there was no left to speak of. The very familiarity of dictatorship meant that a potential Mussolini would have struggled to distinguish himself from the run-of-the-mill macho military ruler and acquire the aura of a saviour.

Brazil was something of an exception. Getúlio Varga's overthrow of the oligarchic 'Old Republic' in 1930 occurred at a time of crisis caused by the collapse of prices for coffee, Brazil's main source of income. The ensuing economic and social dislocation ushered in a period of polarization between communists and the fascistic Integralists. The latter, with at least 200,000 members, rejected traditional Brazilian liberalism in favour of nationalism, antisemitism, and anticommunism. They sought to weld the country's diverse ethnicities into a Brazilian race defined in historical and cultural terms. They wanted to replace a system based on patronage with one of loyalty to nation and regime. They anticipated the dream of the mobilized nation in the usual fascist rituals, salutes, and shirts (green in this case).

Like fascists in Romania and Hungary, the Integralists came into conflict with an increasingly dictatorial regime. In 1937 Varga established a frankly authoritarian 'New State', in alliance with the coffee-planter elite and urban middle classes. The Integralists were dissolved. They had been unable to establish a party broad enough to compete with Varga's manipulation of patronage. Neither were they able to match the Eastern European fascists' appeal to the rural poor, who remained in thrall to planters.

The one Latin American regime that has sometimes been considered fascist is the Perón dictatorship in Argentina. The country was more advanced than most Latin American states, and had a long tradition of radical rightism, which owed something to the conservative Catholic nationalism of France and Spain. Juan Domingo Perón began as labour minister in the military regime of General José Uriburu – another of the dictatorships that admired Mussolini and Hitler. In 1943, in a bid to provide the Uriburu regime, which didn't have the unanimous support of the wealthy, with popular support, Perón turned to the trade unions. He negotiated a deal, according to which the government implemented trade union demands concerning welfare and income redistribution, while the unions backed Perón's bid for international pre-eminence. This combination of nationalism and socialism, together with Perón's admiration for Mussolini, and the attempt to organize a single party, has led many to view this unusual regime as fascist. Yet the fact that Perón had not come to power at the head of a mass party meant that one finds none of the attempted undermining of the existing state structures that was so characteristic of fascism. The Perónist regime also left room for opposition – it was neither totalitarian nor fascist.

Chapter 7
Phoenix from the ashes?

Ur-Fascism [a term meaning 'eternal fascism'] is still around us, sometimes in plainclothes. It would be so much easier for us, if there appeared on the scene somebody saying, 'I want to reopen Auschwitz, I want the Blackshirts to parade again in the Italian squares'. Life is not that simple. Ur-Fascism can come back under the most innocent of disguises. Our duty is to uncover it and point the finger at any of its new instances – every day and in every part of the world.

Umberto Eco, 'Ur-Fascism' in *The New York Review of Books*, 22 June 1995

Stirring as Umberto Eco's words are to defenders of freedom, they won't do as a means of understanding fascism in the contemporary world. If it were possible for fascism to dress 'in plainclothes', how could we tell which of the myriad political movements around us was fascist? Should we look at those which most resemble our idea of fascism, or those which least resemble it?

Eco breaks one of the fundamental rules of academic enquiry (and indeed of any fruitful exchange between people). To be useful to scholars a proposition must be *falsifiable* – there must be something which could in theory refute the statement. No evidence could contradict Eco's view that a movement was fascist. If one said that such and such essential characteristic was missing from the movement in question, the rejoinder would always be 'Ah! They're keeping their intentions secret!' This kind of logic lies behind all conspiracy theories, with their infuriating imperviousness to counter-argument.

Having said that, Eco does put his finger on a difficulty regarding the analysis of the contemporary extreme right. With the exception of the Italian Social Movement (MSI), none of the parties that explicitly seek to restore Fascist or Nazi states (as they believe them to have existed) has ever been electorally significant. For that reason, such movements do not figure in this chapter; our concern is with parties that have enjoyed a degree of success, but that have rejected the fascist label.

At what point does a movement that abandons some of the key features of fascism cease to be usefully described as fascist? We might find evidence that a movement consciously attempts to dupe the electorate in the interests of obtaining power. In other cases we won't. Even where we do find such evidence, we still have to take into account the fact that hundreds of thousands of people vote for parties in the conviction that they are not fascist, and might not have done so had they thought that they were.

To resolve the problem we must return to the question of definition. A concept can be elaborated according to which cases we wish to include. If we want to include marginal cases, we simply widen the definition a little. Yet there is a cost, in that the definition's sharpness is reduced. Watering down our definition of fascism highlights similarities between historic fascism and the contemporary extreme right. But we have to leave out important features of the definition, such as hostility to electoral democracy and paramilitarism. The price of doing so is that the distinctiveness of historic fascism, and especially what differentiated it from other movements at the time, becomes harder to pin down.

To my mind, the cost of weakening the definition of fascism to include the contemporary extreme right is too great. One alternative would be to use the term 'neo-fascist'. It has the beauty of familiarity, and rightly in many cases reveals a deliberate attempt to make fascism relevant in new conditions. This term has the potential disadvantage, however, of obscuring some fundamental differences between fascism and contemporary forms of the extreme right. Whereas fascism sees the destruction of democracy as a precondition for the triumph of ultranationalism, the contemporary extreme right attempts to ethnically homogenize democracy and reserve its advantages for the dominant nationality. Their imagined society is perhaps closer to the South African Apartheid state or to the ideals of white separatists in the United States. I prefer to use the term 'national-populist' to describe this form of movement.

This is not to deny the existence of a great number of movements explicitly inspired by Nazism and Fascism. An American investigator's conversation with Charles Hall, commander of the White Aryan Legion, revealed something of the psychology of those who adhere to such movements.

> You know, a true white separatist – a true National Socialist . . . always felt the same way. Was always attracted to the swastika, to the iron cross and stuff . . . The swastika without doubt is the most hated symbol, but it should be the most loved and cherished symbol there is . . . When you put . . . a swastika on your skin or you wear it on your shirt, you've separated yourself from 99.9 percent of the population.
>
> Quoted in Betty E. Dobratz and Stephanie L. Shanks-Meile, *'White Power, White Pride': The White Separatist Movement in the United States*

However violent they are, such movements deliberately reject mainstream politics and society. So long as Nazi regalia triggers revulsion in the majority, such movements have little prospect of entering the political mainstream. In the United States, for example, there were no more than 10,000–20,000 members of the overtly racist extreme right. Our concern is with movements that have attempted to overcome the discredit and marginalization of fascism.

From fascism to national-populism

In 1945 fascism was deeply discredited, and most post-war regimes (in both Eastern and Western Europe) owed their very legitimacy to the struggle against fascism. West German and Italian democracies were ruled by Christian democrats and socialists who rejected open expressions of sympathy for fascism. In such circumstances it was nearly impossible for explicitly fascist parties to gain a toehold. In Germany, although opinion polls revealed that many people felt Nazism to have been a good idea badly carried out, neo-Nazis have so far achieved only regional successes. The German constitution forbids the formation of antidemocratic parties, and Christian Democrat governments have been prepared to ban fascist organizations. Throughout the post-war years, the German economic miracle, coupled with conservative Christian Democrat government, have ensured that no party was in a position to break these bans. When in 1960 an Italian Christian Democrat government accepted the votes of neo-fascist deputies in order to remain in office, massive demonstrations forced the prime minister to resign. (Even in Spain after 1945 Christian democrats and monarchists increased their influence at the expense of fascists within Franco's regime because of fear of foreign condemnation.) Furthermore, since fascism was associated in the popular mind with ultranationalism, it was difficult for the extreme right to get around popular antipathy by changing its name – a party might be fascist without using the label, but it would cease to be so without ultranationalism.

The story of the Italian Social Movement (MSI) – for decades the most significant European extreme right party – is illustrative of the problems faced by fascists. Founded in 1946, the MSI unashamedly assumed Mussolini's mantle and at first was directed by Fascists living clandestinely. It survived only because Italy did not possess a credible democratic conservative party. Most conservative voters backed the centrist Christian Democrats out of fear that supporting a right-wing party would divide the centre and let the Communists into government. Those conservatives who refused to back the Christian Democrats voted for the MSI, or for the equally marginal monarchists.

Even now, fascism remains a term of abuse. Yet extreme-right politics are once more espoused by significant minorities, for antifascism no longer structures the political landscape so profoundly. Generational turnover rendered the antifascist reference 'mechanical', so that the term fascism remains taboo, but the ideas associated with it are less so. The student uprisings of 1968 inadvertently weakened antifascism further. Student radicals ridiculed what they saw as their elders' cynical manipulation of antifascism in order to legitimate their own power. Students indiscriminately accused contemporary governments of fascism, and helped empty the term of useful content.

The second reason for the greater acceptability of extreme-right politics is that right-wing intellectuals have redefined ultranationalism. In effect, they have translated xenophobia and intolerance into liberal-democratic language. A crucial role was played by the French thinker Alain de Benoist, and the 'New Right' of the 1970s. The New Right represented a reaction against the student movement of 1968, but (typically of fascism) it combined traditional sources of right-wing inspiration with the ideas of certain left-wing thinkers.

The New Right set out to undermine the universalist values of liberal democracy. Much of their output was not new – one has no difficulty in recognizing an updating of the pseudo-science that inspired inter-war fascism (the inevitable struggle between nations, the survival of the fittest, the necessary inequality of individuals, the need for racial purity). What was original (or almost so, for the radical Nazi Otto Strasser had espoused similar ideas) was the use of 'equal rights' to justify discrimination against minorities within states – in order to preserve the alleged distinctiveness of a given nation, it was necessary to restrict the rights of those who were said to threaten the identity of the majority. The New Right reasserted the alleged spiritual uniqueness of European nations against the globalizing tendencies of American capitalism and multiculturalism. Henceforth it was possible for the far right to deny that it was racist – 'we fight only for the equal rights of all nations to exist' – whilst preaching the need for discrimination against minorities. The far right could connect with the 'I'm not racist, but . . . ' tendency which is so prevalent in contemporary society.

It was not immediately obvious that this updating of ultranationalism would pay dividends, for the New Right appealed only to a small (but Europe-wide) group of intellectuals. Moreover, the circumstances in which, in 1983–4, the French National Front (FN) broke into mass politics recalled the conditions in which fascism had flourished in inter-war Europe. In 1981, in the midst of a global economic crisis, the French Socialists had captured the presidency and for the first time ever formed a government based entirely on a left-wing majority. The right, meanwhile, had begun a descent into quarrelsome factions from which it has not yet emerged, and some conservatives blamed previous right-wing governments for favouring trade unions and liberalizing morals (notably through the legalization of abortion). There was, moreover, a tradition of political racism in France. After the war this had been directed at North Africans (often by the descendants of Italians and Spaniards who had once been the targets of anti-immigrant feeling themselves). This racism was reinforced by the memory of France's withdrawal from its North African empire in 1963 following a bitter war. Hence the resonance of FN leader Le Pen's depiction of North Africans as a 'foreign army camped on French soil'.

At first, the FN electorate was relatively bourgeois, elderly, Catholic, conservative, and antisocialist. The Party programme coincided with this electorate's demands for deregulation and a return to the free market (this was the decade of Ronald Reagan and Margaret Thatcher). The Arab became a symbol of the 'unfit' who vegetated on welfare benefits. The FN represented a mobilization of discontented bourgeois conservatives who blamed their leaders for the advance of socialism, feminism, and immigration.

In subsequent years, the FN has become more of an all-class party. Most interestingly, it has become *the* party of the young, working-class male, often unemployed, relatively uneducated, living in the industrial suburbs of large cities. Astonishingly, in the presidential elections of 1995, 30% of workers voted for the FN, more than voted for the socialists or the communists. These characteristics of the FN can be seen in extreme-right parties elsewhere in Europe.

What has happened? Decades of unemployment amongst unskilled young men, thanks to the de-industrialization of Western economies, is one obvious reason. Traditional industry has disappeared from Western economies, to be replaced by unskilled temporary jobs often filled by women. For different reasons, Russia and the former East Germany have also witnessed the collapse of heavy industry and agriculture under the impact of free market reforms, and these sectors provide much support for the extreme right. Work no longer provides identity and status for many young men in Western societies. Given that in these same societies there is ever more pressure to consume conspicuously, and that consumer goods are linked to sex appeal, poor young men feel left out. They resent the wealthy, and dislike career women. In ghettoized suburban estates, young white men are involved in confrontations with immigrants, whom they blame for crime and attacks on 'their' women. National-populist racism, recast as the defence of oppressed 'minorities' against multiculturalism, appeals especially in these areas. Of course, poor whites are actually underprivileged members of the *dominant* ethnic group, and as such they command a greater degree of sympathy from the police and press than do immigrants. It is, however, perceptions that matter.

Perceptions matter so much that it is not just the poor workers of urban ghettos who have turned to racist politics, but prosperous workers too, as the advance of the national-populists in wealthy Switzerland, Austria, and Denmark illustrates. In Denmark Pia Kjaersgaard won 22 seats in 2001 by denouncing an Islamic invasion, even though the Muslim population is lower in Denmark than anywhere else in Europe. Poverty alone, even coupled with the presence of immigrants, doesn't explain the rise of national-populism.

Another important issue is that during the 1990s socialist and communist parties in East and West Europe have abandoned much of their former radicalism. The differences between left and right have been attenuated, and all parties speak largely for those who have gained from the transformation of the economy, leaving the losers without representation. As the left has shifted rightwards in search of electoral success, conservative parties have often adopted xenophobic populism in order to differentiate themselves from the left. Not to be outdone, the left reassures the electorate that it is not soft on immigrants either. Anti-immigrant policies become respectable, and the extreme right's ultranationalism appears relevant.

It is all the more so since ultranationalism can be presented as a defence of unique national cultures against 'globalization' – evident in the increasing internationalization of the economy, immigration flows, the ubiquity of Coca-Cola, and the removal of tariff protection for farmers. The extreme right takes up the causes of all those whose difficulties can be attributed to globalization. In Glasgow and Moscow the extreme right denounces McDonalds and attacks Afghan immigrants. In Western Europe the far right castigates the European Union (EU) as an agent of globalization. The possibility that the EU might incorporate the new democracies of Eastern Europe reinforces fear of a new wave of immigration from the east.

Actually, globalization is not new, for nation-states have always had to reckon with the internationalizing tendencies of capitalism, technological change, and advanced communications. Periodically, politicians invoke globalization in order to justify their policies ('accept lower wages, or we won't be able to compete internationally and you will lose your job!'). Movements of various political persuasions have protested against globalization. As ultranationalists, fascists joined in. Back in the 1880s, the radical right saw the Jewish Rothschild bank as the personification of the occult power of cosmopolitan finance capital – a danger to honest national business and upright native workers. We cannot therefore see national-populism as an 'automatic' reaction to globalization. We have to ask why globalization is perceived as important at this particular time. The answer is that in a changing political landscape it intersects with problems caused by deindustrialization, structural unemployment, and ethnic rivalries – at a time when the New Right rendered globalization politically useful. The defence of 'identity' has enabled neo-fascists to mobilize a socially more mixed coalition than that which supported fascists in the 1930s.

The fact that the circumstances that produced national-populism differ from those from which inter-war fascism issued does not necessarily disqualify the former from being fascist. Once the idea of fascism is 'out there' it is potentially available for use in a variety of situations. One can make educated guesses as to the circumstances in which it might emerge, but there is no predicting the precise circumstances in which it will become a mass movement. To answer our central question – to what extent does national-populism resemble historic fascism? – we have to look at what the extreme right does and says too.

Italy: from national-populism to post-fascism

For the first half-century of its existence, the MSI wrestled with the contradictions of the fascist heritage. It drew its social programme – corporatism, workers' participation in management, and some nationalization of key industries – from the radical wing of Fascism. Its political programme was more moderate: a presidential constitution close to the US model. This caution stemmed from fear of repression if it embraced illegality, and from the influence of conservatives within the party. The latter, without, it must be stressed, repudiating the Fascist heritage, were convinced that the MSI would best succeed in alliance with conventional conservatives. Usually, 'moderates' managed to fend off the challenge from the radicals, for the party did best electorally amongst the descendants of southern conservatives who had rallied to Mussolini after the conquest of power. In the 1960s and 1970s some frustrated radicals split off and engaged in a campaign of terrorist provocation. Whichever faction was dominant, the MSI failed to win more than about 9% of the vote – usually much less.

In October 1992 the MSI celebrated the 70th anniversary of the March on Rome with parades, Roman salutes, and songs. That year, however, witnessed a fundamental change in the movement's position. This was precipitated first by the collapse of communism, which caused the powerful Italian Communist Party to transform itself into a moderate democratic socialist movement, thereby depriving the extreme right of its main enemy. Secondly, there was the emergence in 1992 of the Northern League under Umberto Bossi. This movement was dedicated to winning the autonomy of the 'productive' north from the 'African' south, a prospect that caused the MSI to discover an attachment to the Italian state. Thirdly, in 1992–3, the hitherto dominant Christian Democrats imploded under the impact of fraud investigations. Antifascism ceased to be the touchstone of political acceptability, and electoral space opened on the right, into which the MSI stepped.

By this time the moderate Gianfranco Fini had recaptured the party from radicals, and a new generation of party officials without personal links to Fascism rose to prominence. Fini's change of priorities was more fundamental than previous efforts to capture moderate opinion. He made symbolic gestures of reconciliation with the resistance tradition, which in the past had been dismissed as worthless. Dictatorship was repudiated, and democracy accepted as a system of values. Fascist racial legislation was disavowed. The reformed MSI gave Italy what it had never previously had – a self-consciously right-wing Catholic conservative party. It might also be said to represent a return to the roots of southern conservatives.

In 1995 the MSI confirmed these changes by transforming itself into the Alleanza Nationale (AN). A year earlier the movement had gained 14% of the vote and entered the government of the media mogul Silvio Berlusconi. This government soon collapsed, thanks partly to struggles between Bossi and Fini. In 2001 Fini returned to government as deputy prime minister, the AN having won 12% of the vote.

Certainly, the AN has a debt to Fascism – its use of the term 'post-fascist' to describe itself is meant to acknowledge this. The party's radical wing still exists, and shows a degree of sympathy for the skinhead politics of football hooliganism. Like fascists everywhere, it cites revolutionaries of left and right as its ideological inspiration – in this case the Communist Antonio Gramsci and Italy's answer to Heinrich Himmler, Julius Evola, both of whom had been cited by the French New Right. Again following the New Right, the AN rejects the idea that races are unequal, yet sees immigration as a threat to national identity. In 2001 Fini revived fears of Fascist censorship by demanding a commission to purge school textbooks of 'Marxist bias' (distorting Mussolini's war record was one such offence). It has been claimed that the AN has 'bypassed' its fascist heritage by depriving its still-fascistic activists of a voice in party affairs, rather than subjecting fascism to critique.

To see the AN as fascist, however, would require a definition so broad that it would render impossible any distinction between conventional conservatism and fascism, let alone between fascism and conservative dictatorships. In fact the Berlusconi coalition's most extreme element is Umberto Bossi, who is obsessed with immigration and believes the EU to be run by paedophiles. Fini's law-and-order, anti-immigrant, anti-European Union politics were scarcely harsher than those of Berlusconi himself.

The French National Front

The French National Front (FN) is a different kettle of fish. It was formed in 1972 as an umbrella organization – a front – for several organizations that wanted to exploit immigration as an electoral issue. As their leader they chose Jean-Marie Le Pen, whose views were perhaps a little too conservative for many hard-line fascists. His relative moderation did not, however, turn the FN into a mass party until 1983, when the party won 17% of the vote in the municipal elections in the town of Dreux. By the mid-1990s the Front was gaining over 15% in national elections and had captured a small number of significant municipal governments. Following a split in the party between Le Pen and his heir apparent Bruno Mégret in early 1999 many observers predicted the end of the FN. Yet Le Pen managed to hold on to the FN's name, and showed in the 2001 municipal elections that he was some way ahead of Mégret. In the Presidential elections of April 2002 Le Pen achieved a modest increase in his vote compared to 1995, while the addition of Mégret's votes took the extreme right to no less than 20% of the vote. Thanks to the division of the left, Le Pen's score was sufficient to place him second to incumbent President Jacques Chirac and earn him the right to confront the latter in the run-off ballot.

What sort of movement is the FN? Like the Italian AN, the FN consciously attempts to render the extreme right more acceptable to 'moderate' opinion. But there the resemblance ends. Whereas Fini has made gestures of reconciliation with antifascists, Le Pen has aroused suspicions that he sympathizes with the 'revisionist' view of the Holocaust (that is, with those who say that it didn't happen). The Front follows the New Right in denying racism, yet advocates the repatriation of immigrants in the name of defence of national identity. Its social policy is summed up in the term 'national preference', which means giving priority in housing, welfare benefits, and education to French people. All of this recalls fascism.

The Front's economic policy is harder to assess. During the 1980s, the FN espoused extreme free-market liberalism, whereas fascism typically favoured corporatism and regulation. Those who see the FN as fascist might point to Mussolini's embracing of the free market during his first years in office. More convincingly, Mussolini's liberal period could be seen as the result of compromise with conservatives and as evidence that at this stage the regime was far from fascist. Acceptance of the free market represents a major watering-down of fascism. Free-market ideology may permit the suppression of free trade unions, but it means dropping the desire to subordinate the economy to the national interest, with all the consequences this entails. So long as free-market economics remained dominant in the FN it could not be truly fascist. As it turns out, however, the FN did adopt corporatist politics in the 1990s.

There is another problem regarding the nature of the FN. Unlike historic fascism, the FN does not oppose democracy. On the contrary, the movement's declared goal is to reinforce the sovereignty of the people through the use of the referendum and the restoration of the powers of parliament (in France under the Fifth Republic real power lies with the executive). These reforms, it is said, will loosen the grip on power of unelected technocrats and establishment politicians, and allow the real wishes of the people concerning immigration, the death penalty, and 'national preference' to be heard. So far as it goes, this programme can be seen as a form of democracy – or rather it exploits the too-widespread identification of democracy with the absolute enforcement of the will of the majority. The FN's conception of democracy is therefore inseparable from its racist project. It assumes that once in power it would be possible to win referendums on the main planks of its programme. Unlike historic fascists, the FN does not demand an end to competitive elections, and there's no evidence that it intends to establish a permanent dictatorship.

Neither has Le Pen attempted to use party violence to lever himself into power. The suggestion that the FN follows Hitler and Mussolini in seeking power constitutionally rests on the mistaken assumption that these dictators gained power legally. They didn't. They openly attacked liberal democracy, and used violent paramilitary movements to coerce conservatives, albeit not entirely unsympathetic to fascism, into accepting them as coalition partners. Mussolini's speech to parliament of 16 November 1922 exemplified the Fascists' mixture of conciliation and threat.

The FN does not possess a mass paramilitary wing comparable to those of historic fascists. There are certainly elements within the party who would like to create such a movement. The FN includes many skinheads and other elements who are ever-ready to resort to violence. But there is no sign that majority opinion in the FN sees the party as the nucleus of a militarized, one-party state. One could, perhaps, object that national-populism has recognized that in modern society paramilitarism and one-party rule are impossible and have developed other means to the same end. Yet once again, the abandonment of paramilitarism is no small matter, for it is not just a secondary feature of fascism. The fact that Hitler's and Mussolini's conquest of power depended on the pressure of their armed followers was crucial for the histories of their regimes. How different would the history of fascism have been if Mussolini's Blackshirts or Hitler's SA and SS had not aspired to take over some of the functions of the civil service, police, and army? Radical fascists may have failed to achieve all their ends, but we would make little sense of fascism in inter-war Europe if we regarded any of this as secondary.

The FN might have started from the intention of rendering fascism more acceptable, yet by stripping it of dictatorship, one-party rule, and paramilitarism, it has become something rather different. In my view, the FN represents a form of racist national-populism. It appeals, or attempts to appeal, directly to the people, over the heads of a corrupt establishment, in order to implement illiberal exclusionist policies.

The extreme right in Russia

The resurgence of the extreme right in Russia, nine decades after the heyday of the Black Hundreds, is no surprise. Here was a country where the left had collapsed and where the liberal-democratic economic reforms of Boris Yeltsin created massive discontent. Russia, moreover, had lost its empire, been humiliated in Afghanistan, and seemed to be at the mercy of the West. Like inter-war Germans and Italians, Russians were exercised by the fate of fellow nationals in neighbouring republics.

In December 1993, Vladimir Zhirinovsky's absurdly named Liberal Democratic Party won around 25% of the party preference votes in elections to the Duma (parliament). Zhirinovsky is a flamboyant character, part showman, part fantasist, and part extreme nationalist. His style is typical of fascist male chauvinism. Casting his vote, he told foreign journalists 'Political impotence is finished. Today is the beginning of the orgasm. All the people, I promise you, will feel the orgasm of next year's [presidential elections]'. Zhirinovsky's message was simple. Placing his faith in the Russian people and the Russian spirit, he would raise Russia from its knees. He promised restoration of the Russian empire and attacked foreigners and Jews.

Contrary to expectation, 1993 was the beginning of the end for Zhirinovsky. In subsequent elections his vote has not reached double figures. The reason is plain – other parties have taken over his policies. The most interesting of these is the reconstituted Russian Communist Party under Gennady Zyuganov, which has been reinvented as an ultranationalist movement. Zyuganov does not reject all of communist history, for Soviet communism always contained a national-populist hatred of the rich. He admires Lenin and Stalin for having preserved the Russian state in the face of civil war and foreign invasion respectively, and calls for a new struggle against the West. Marxism, however, has been dumped in favour of spiritual nationalism – communism is criticized for having made too many concessions to Western materialism, and the Orthodox Church is enthroned as the embodiment of Russian history. Zyuganov claims to speak for the Russian people, and for the genuine party activist, against foreign-controlled fat cats like Gorbachev and Yeltsin. He declares himself 'Russian in his blood, culture, and psychology', and boasts of never having had a serious conversation with a woman. In sum, Zyuganov reconciles nationalism and communism.

Dare we call this national socialism? Perhaps. There is certainly much here that resembles fascism, especially as it remains uncertain whether the still powerful Communist Party apparatus wants to recover its role in the government of the country. Yet it remains difficult to advocate frankly a return to dictatorship in Russia. Like Le Pen, Zyuganov is reluctant to break entirely with the market economy or with democracy. He wants to retain the multi-party system, and to increase the powers of parliament (not least because the National Communists are strong there).

The National Communists won (so far as that is possible in Russia's confused political system) the parliamentary elections of December 1995, yet despite a strong showing failed to oust Yeltsin in the presidential elections of the following year. Having deprived Zhirinovsky of his electorate, the National Communists themselves were subsequently outflanked by Vladimir Putin, became prime minister in 1999 and president in 2000. The previously unknown Putin won massive popularity by fighting a vicious war against Chechen separatists and by posing as a man of action. A black-belt in Judo, he was once thrown to the floor (collar and tie and all) in a demonstration match during a state visit to Japan.

Putin describes himself as 'a democrat – a Russian democrat'. He is not a fascist. But his success does show that there is a fund of populism in Russia, a politics of 'us against them', which was once harnessed to communism and has now been appropriated by ultranationalists.

The far right in the United States

The United States is another country in which a well-rooted populism is capable of being turned to the far right. Here, the origins of the extreme right were to be found in the ranks of the disillusioned of both main parties. White Southern Democrats resented the role of the Democrat administrations of the 1960s in enforcing civil rights legislation. The KKK once again expanded in this period, and some members backed the avowedly racist dissident Democrat George Wallace's presidential bid in 1968. Disillusioned Southern voters then turned to Ronald Reagan's Republicans in 1980. Meanwhile, since the 1950s the right of the Republican Party has denounced its own administrations' alleged failure to have done with the New Deal's interventionist economic policies, and for their supposed softness towards international communism (some believed that President Eisenhower was a Communist puppet). Again, in the late 1960s and early 1970s, the ultraliberal wing of the Republicans attacked President Nixon for his supposedly interventionist economic policies. In the 1970s, this ultraliberal right converged with the Christian fundamentalist movement, which saw family and Christian schools as under attack by the state. There were some incompatibilities between these three components of the right – economic liberals, for example, disliked Southerners' predilection for high spending on white voters. Nevertheless, the two latter tendencies, with some themes borrowed from the first, were extremely influential during the presidency of Ronald Reagan (1980–8).

Perhaps predictably, Reagan did not satisfy his radical supporters. Abortion was not abolished, prayers were not introduced into schools, and some disliked his willingness to negotiate with Gorbachev. His successor, George Bush, worsened discontent by raising taxes. More radical forms of rightism emerged, with Pat Robertson's campaign for the Republican nomination in 1988. Radical rightism remained within the Republican party with Newt Gringrich's *Contract With America* campaign of 1994, and with Pat Buchanan's campaigns for the party's nomination in 1992 and 1996. Soon the cycle of hope and disappointment had set in again, and discontent moved outside the established right. Buchanan ran as candidate for the Reform Party in the 2000 presidential election. He espoused all the traditional right-wing causes, such as anti-abortion and prayers in schools, and he decried the feminist and gay rights movements. Buchanan also revived the right's old opposition to US entanglement in world affairs. He saw Bush's announcement of a 'New World Order' as a betrayal of American interests to the big corporations and the partisans of globalization, and accused free-trading governments of neglecting the interests of American workers. Buchanan's campaign had much in common with European national-populist movements. He gained 21% of the vote in the 1996 Republican primaries.

Comparison with the European experience is still more intriguing if we examine another new movement – the militias, or Patriot Movement, which sprouted in the wake of the death of 76 people at Waco, Texas, in February 1993, as a result of the FBI's siege of the headquarters of a religious sect. The militias hold that the armed citizenry of the American Revolution must prevent the federal government from running amok again in the future. Only the gun-toting citizen can defend the original constitution of the American people against a government bent on selling out the country to the global world order, incarnate in the United Nations. Combat-ready UN troops and their black helicopters, it seems, have been sighted on American soil. The original American freedoms, moreover, were held only by whites, and were never intended for blacks.

The militias differ from European national-populists in that they are strongly libertarian. They deny the government's right to issue drivers' licences or tax the people. Some claim that the government infringes the true meaning of the constitution, others that the constitution itself was an imposition upon free Americans, and even that the constitution is a cover for the continued rule of the US by the British monarchy and its ally, international finance. This hostility to a pro-globalization federal government in the name of an ethnically pure nation recalls that of European national-populists to the European Union.

Conclusion

Our case studies show that those who candidly assumed the legacy of fascism were rarely able to enter mainstream politics. Those who have sought to render the extreme right acceptable in an age assumed to be democratic have moved in radically different directions. Fini's AN has become a democratic conservative party – albeit in a context in which mainstream European conservatism has become markedly more right-wing. At the other extreme, Germany's violent far-right parties, with their large skinhead memberships and history of anti-immigrant violence, have struggled to make an impact. The reformed East German communist movement (more left-wing than its Russian counterpart) has largely monopolized protests against economic problems in the east, and while many Germans dislike immigrants, they fear neo-Nazis even more. In late 2001 it was feared that frustrated fascists were turning to terrorism.

The most successful of fascism's heirs, like the FN, have transformed themselves into racist and populist parties operating within democratic legality. With some variations, this applies to Jörg Haider's Freedom Party (FPÖ), which won second place in the Austrian general election of October 1999. The FPÖ combines extreme free-market policies with tough policies on law and order (including routine drug tests for teachers), hostility to immigration, targeting of family allowances and other benefits to Austrian nationals, and antipathy to the Socialists and Christian Democrats who have monopolized power for decades. Christoph Blocher's Swiss People's Party, which gained 22% of the vote in 1999, shares many features of the FPÖ.

All of these parties differ from inter-war fascism in that they issue as much from a crisis of the left as from a crisis of the right. In Russia a left-wing party has turned to the extreme right, whereas in the West it's more a case of young men who might once have been expected to vote for the left looking instead to the extreme right.

The national-populist right is the product of a conscious effort to update fascism, and render it viable in changed conditions. The result is some real continuities (extreme nationalism and discrimination against ethnic minorities, antifeminism, antisocialism, populism, hostility to established social and political elites, anticapitalism, and antiparliamentarianism) coupled with equally significant changes (rejection of mass mobilization, systematic paramilitary violence, and the ambition to create a one-party state). The absent features are precisely those which gave fascism its totalitarian character – summed up in the desire for permanent acclamation of the nation and regime. National-populists have significantly modified their inheritance – in effect, they seek to exploit the racist potential of democracy rather than overthrow it. This is not to say that national-populism is somehow 'less evil', or 'less dangerous', than fascism. That is another question altogether.

Chapter 8
Fascism, nation, and race

As an ultranationalist ideology, fascism is unabashedly racist. Fascists do not treat all inhabitants of the territory as citizens, or as human beings possessed of equal rights. Citizenship and its benefits are accorded or denied on the basis of conformity to, or possession of, characteristics alleged to be 'national', be they biological, cultural, religious, or political. Nationalism and racism pervade all aspects of fascist practice, from welfare provision and family policy to diplomacy. Those deemed to be outside the nation face an uncertain future – extermination in the worst case.

Historic fascists were quite open about the superiority of their own nation, and happily used the category 'race'. Contemporary national-populists are more reluctant to describe themselves as racists, for the term has slipped into such disrepute that no one who pretends to be decent can adopt the label. Like the South African Apartheid regime, they conceal their bigotry behind the notion that races (like genders) are 'equal but different'. Cursory examination reveals such distinctions to be phoney. Yet the relationship between fascism and racism is nevertheless complex.

Biological and cultural racism

First we have to make some distinctions. The most inflexible form of racism holds that race is determined biologically. Biological destiny cannot be changed, and assimilation into another nationality is impossible. Indeed, the Nazis believed assimilated Jews to be more dangerous, for they acted secretly. Biological racism also divides peoples into higher and lower, the latter not clearly distinct from higher animals. These 'sub-humans' might be used in the interests of the higher races, or even killed.

National identity is not always biologically defined. In the early 20th century educated Europeans usually understood race in terms of history and culture. An individual belonged to a nation if she or he inhabited the nation's historic territory, spoke the national language, or practised its religion. This racism is less extreme in that it allows for 'assimilation' by learning the national language or changing one's religion. Sometimes assimilation has been associated with projects regarded as progressive: in liberal 19th-century France and Hungary, Jews gained full civil rights – so long as they refrained from public displays of difference. In Soviet Russia, Jews climbed to the top of the governmental tree, yet the regime ruthlessly stamped out expressions of Jewish culture.

Nevertheless, assimilationism rests on racist assumptions: one cannot be a citizen possessed of equal rights unless one conforms to the supposed cultural characteristics of the majority. A genuinely liberal position accepts religious, linguistic, and cultural diversity, and even emotional identification with other states, provided the inhabitant obeys a law equally applicable to all. Even more importantly, all those presumed to have broken the law are treated in the same way. No one is regarded as more likely to have committed a crime because of their ethnic origins. All have the same entitlement to 'due process'. For liberals there are no 'loyalty tests', such as knowledge of the nation's history or support for the national football team.

Assimilationism is especially discriminatory where it involves oppressive measures such as the closure of minority language schools, as it often did in inter-war Europe. Much depends too on the amount of time said to be required before an individual is assimilated. Barrès assumed that the peasantry imbibed Frenchness through *centuries* of contact with the national soil. He held, moreover, that Jews were urban creatures who could never be fully French because they had never tilled the soil. This 'blood and soil' nationalism was widely prevalent on the European right, fascist and non-fascist, in the inter-war years. Since it left little scope for ethnic minorities to change their national belonging, it was potentially as exclusive as Nazi racism.

The differences between biological and historical/cultural racism are blurred further by the Nazis' forced assimilation of populations they regarded as racially close to Germans. The National Socialist People's Welfare Organization (NSV) forcibly resettled in Germany Dutch and Norwegian mothers of children born of German fathers. The NSV even kidnapped children from Polish orphanages, and endeavoured to Germanize them through discipline and forced labour. Nazi 'experts' debated the assimilability of particular populations in learned journals – thereby giving an air of scientific respectability to their policies.

There is thus a continuum between liberal assimilationism, forced assimilation, exclusionist and exterminationist racism. Fascism won't tolerate diversity of identities, or the notion that a person can simultaneously fulfil her or his duties as a citizen and espouse other identities. But fascism can be positioned anywhere on this scale.

Another complication is that racism has never been the monopoly of the right or extreme right. Racist assumptions, sometimes explicit, sometimes unconscious, have often informed left-wing thought and practice too. The history of left-wing racism lies outside the scope of this book, but it is worth pointing out that left-wing racism differs from fascism in important respects. The left has usually been optimistic about the possibility of assimilation, and it has rarely believed that racial policy was a panacea for society's ills. By definition, socialists believe class to be more important than race.

Nazism

The case of Nazism might seem straightforward, were it not for the fact that certain of the approaches deployed by academics have diminished the significance of racism in Nazism. Marxists tended to view antisemitism as a means for capitalists to hide the real causes of workers' misery. Weberians argued that the Jew was a convenient symbol of the modern world that fascists disliked so much. These interpretations are not invalid, but racism was more than a device to achieve other ends.

More recent interpretations of Nazism have demonstrated that race pervaded all aspects of Nazism. Hitler himself adhered to all the premises of politicized biological racism. In *Mein Kampf* he sorted races into a hierarchy with Aryans at the summit, assumed that there was a Darwinian struggle for domination between races, and argued that there was a will to purity within each race. Individuals and social groups gained fulfilment through self-sacrifice for the good of the race.

For Hitler, the Jews were engaged in a permanent struggle to undermine the Aryan race, especially by promoting cosmopolitan capitalism and communism, and encouraging war between 'healthy' nations. Hitler also saw prostitution as a means for Jews to corrupt Aryans through transmission of syphilis. Indeed, all hereditary diseases were said to be spread by Jews. Hence his advocacy of eugenicist solutions to the racial question: selective breeding, sterilization of the unfit, welfare legislation for the sound elements of the population, and encouragement of healthy women to reproduce. Hitler did not speak of extermination, but the language he used to describe Jews – bacilli, leeches, parasites – could, and did, legitimate extermination. Antisemitism, eugenicism, anticapitalism, and anticommunism were different aspects of the same policy.

Historians have rightly pointed to the fact that during the Nazis' rise to power, as part of their bid for conservative support, the Jews were only one of several enemies attacked by the Nazis (others included the Poles, Catholics, Communists, and socialists), and that since the Jews were perceived to pose no immediate threat, they were not usually the primary target of Nazis at this time. Yet antisemitism was literally an obsession with Hitler and his chief henchmen. Antisemitism was also a significant, but subtle, part of Nazi propaganda all along. The 1931 programme for the peasantry spoke of the need for racial struggle against the advancing east (read Judeo-Bolshevism) and demanded a law to protect the peasantry as 'the source of blood renewal of the German people'. Capitalists were conventionally portrayed with caricatured Jewish features. Antisemitism was intrinsic to anticommunism too. Take the poster from the 1932 presidential elections reproduced in Figure 7. The top part of the poster depicts a variety of socialists and Communists under the caption, in pseudo-Hebraic lettering, 'We are voting for Hindenburg!' The pictures beneath, under a heading in traditional Germanic script, are of leading Nazis who will be voting for Hitler. Other posters portray demonic Communists with devilish Jews whispering in their ears.

Although the extermination of the Jews was not inevitable at the time of the seizure of power, the Nazis set about implementing their racist designs as soon as they won power. The great credit earned by Hitler as victor over the communists and architect of Germany's national resurrection permitted him and those who were loyal to him to implement their racist designs. Some of the first measures to follow the passage of the Enabling Act restricted Jewish employment in the civil service and professions. In 1935 Jews were forbidden to marry or to have sexual relations with Aryans. Aside from these explicitly racial laws, other aspects of legislation had racial objectives. The Law for the Prevention of Hereditarily Diseased Progeny (July 1933) permitted compulsory sterilization of certain categories of the population. Incentives to

WIR WÄHLEN HINDENBURG!

Wir wählen Hitler!

Schau Dir diese Köpfe an, und Du weißt,
wohin Du gehörst!

7. 'We're voting for Hitler'. Poster from the 1932 presidential election campaign.

women to devote themselves to home and family were intended to increase the quantity of the racially desirable population. Marriage loans and rewards for large families were refused to 'those of lesser racial value'. In 1935 a certificate of racial fitness was required of all those who wished to marry. Shortly before the war – without any formal legal sanction – there began a programme of killing the psychiatrically ill and mentally handicapped. Once the principle that all regulations were racially conditioned was established, subsequent legislation routinely included racial clauses. All these measures were aspects of a single policy: the creation of a racially pure, physically and mentally healthy population, fit to make war on inferior races and conquer living space in the east.

At this stage, Hitler stated publicly that the fate of the Jews was to be confined to ghettos. In practice the hope was that life would become so uncomfortable for Jews that they would emigrate, but the government's reluctance to let Jews take assets with them, and of foreign governments to accept them, thwarted these hopes. The pogrom of 9–10 November 1938 – *Kristallnacht* – resulted from pressure by Nazi activists coupled with Goebbels' yearning for favour with Hitler. It was followed by state plunder of Jewish wealth. Emigration remained the goal, but ominously the SS was accorded greater power over the Jewish question.

Scholars agree that the final radicalization of Nazi policy towards the Jews was precipitated by war in the east. It must be remembered, though, that war against 'Judeo-Bolshevism' had long been the Nazis' goal. In January 1939 Hitler declared that should Jewish finance succeed in plunging Europe into war, the result wouldn't be 'Bolshevizing of the earth, and thus a victory of Jewry, but the annihilation of the Jewish race in Europe'. Some Nazis still interpreted such outbursts as a legitimation of emigration. Others thought it meant forced emigration to Madagascar or Poland – policies which, it was accepted, would entail many fatalities. Hitler's proclamations also licensed the killing of Jews in occupied Poland, and implementation of a policy of ghettoization, forced labour, and expulsion in December 1939 represented a significant move away from the rules normally

8. A Nazi *Einsatzgruppe* murders Jews at Sniatyn, Poland (now in the Ukraine), 11 May 1943.

governing human behaviour. Then, in preparation for the invasion of Russia, instructions were issued to SS special squads – the *Einsatzgruppen* – to kill Communist officials above an undefined rank, Jews in party and state employment, radicals, saboteurs, propagandists, and others. These orders gave an enormous degree of latitude to the *Einsatzgruppen*, all the more so as it was difficult in practice to establish who was a Jew or a Communist.

The *Einsatzgruppen* murdered hundreds of thousands of Jews in local 'actions'. By the end of the year, as Hitler and his subordinates predicted fulfilment of the prophecy of January 1939, the question was not whether, but where, how, and when the Jews would be killed. In early 1941 it was decided that Jews were either to be worked to death in camps or killed immediately. In total, around six million Jews perished.

It is impossible in a book devoted to the question of fascism to do full justice to the horrors of Nazi racism. All that we can do is acknowledge the restrictions of our approach whilst exploring further the knotty relationship between fascism and racism.

The problem of Italian Fascism

This brings us to the problem of Fascism in Italy, for it has often been argued that it was not racist. Italy had no strong tradition of antisemitism, and there were Jews in prominent positions in the Fascist Party and regime. One of Mussolini's mistresses, Margherita Sarfatti, was Jewish, and in a famous interview in 1930 Mussolini ridiculed biological racism. During the war, Italian occupation authorities in France and Croatia refused to hand over Jews to the Germans. Italy adopted Germany's racial laws in 1938, it is said, only because the regime had become subordinate to Nazism. It is thus often argued that Italian Fascism – and Italians – are free of blame for participation in the Holocaust.

This view requires qualification. If we look at Europe as a whole, we find that 1938 witnessed an outbreak of antisemitism across the whole continent, caused by the war scare precipitated by German designs on Austria and Czechoslovakia. In many countries right-wing opinion accused Jews and Bolsheviks of provoking war. Since these fantasies appeared as frequently in Britain and France, which weren't in the thrall of Nazism, as in Italy, it might be suspected that Italian antisemitism was not simply a superficial copy of the German. In fact, early 20th-century Europe possessed a common fund of political ideas. Whilst racism took different forms in different countries, it was 'available' to fascists everywhere.

What is more, it was difficult to separate historical, cultural, and biological racism on the far right. Italy was no exception to this rule. The desire for a unified national community was fundamental to Fascism in Italy, and although biological racism was not systematically deployed in this quest, the regime did espouse a myth of national pre-eminence, based on the alleged superior qualities of the Italic race, and claimed to have recreated the glories of Ancient Rome. Especially revealing is that Fascist Italy carried out a programme of forced assimilation of the German population of the South Tyrol, annexed by Italy after the Great War. The liberal governments of the time justified their rule over the German majority of the province on economic and military grounds, and accorded Germans considerable autonomy. The Fascist regime took a different line. Deploying anthropological and historical arguments every bit as dubious as those advanced by partisans of unification with Germany, the regime argued that South Tyroleans were Italians who had been Germanized while under the rule of the Habsburg Empire. These speculations legitimated draconian measures such as Italianization of surnames, suppression of German newspapers, compulsory use of Italian in the administration, and closure of private German schools. Hitler, usually quick to defend persecuted Germans outside the Reich, refrained from criticizing this policy because he wished to retain

Mussolini's friendship – he denounced German nationalists in the South Tyrol as 'Jewish and bourgeois elements'. In 1938 Hitler began a programme of resettling South Tyroleans within the Reich. Mussolini stuck to his Italianization plan, however, and resisted resettlement.

The regime also justified its programme of eugenic improvement of the Italian 'race' by the need to compete with 'brown and yellow races'. The policy entailed idealization of healthy rural people, with their centuries-old roots in the Italian soil. The potential significance of this exclusionary definition of nationhood was revealed in 1938, when citizenship granted to Jews after 1919 was revoked. By this time Fascist racism had been made more explicit by the conquest of Abyssinia, during which Mussolini declared that imperial conquest was impossible without 'race consciousness'.

Fascist racism elsewhere

A glance at fascist racism outside Germany and Italy confirms that ultranationalism can take many different forms. In Poland, where the Catholic Church was very strong, it was difficult for fascists, or anyone else, to espouse scientific racist doctrines. Here, racism was based more upon antipathy to Jews as killers of Christ and agents of secularism, liberalism, and socialism, coupled with defence of an allegedly timeless Polish Catholic culture. Romanian fascism was equally religious, and on occasion Legionaries rejected biological racism. Nevertheless, the Legion depicted itself as the emanation of the Dacian peasantry – the original inhabitants of what was to become Romania before the Roman conquest. The Romanian elite was believed to have issued from the Roman or Turko-Greek occupying powers, and to have corrupted the country by favouring Jewish and French influences. By the late 1930s expressions of exterminationist antisemitism were quite common in Romania. Romanian armies in Russia would be quite vicious in their pursuit of Jews.

In those countries occupied by the Nazis, there were usually fascists and others prepared to turn a blind eye to atrocities, or to assist the Nazis in killing Jews. Yet it's unlikely that any of these countries would have launched genocidal programmes of their own volition, not least because fascists rarely governed occupied countries. Authoritarian conservative regimes, with their ambivalence towards antisemitism, were more frequently backed by the Nazis. Whether more attached to religious universalism, or retaining a residual belief in assimilation, conservative dictatorships were generally suspicious of fascist racist extremism. The Hungarian regime resisted Nazi demands to deport its Jewish population until the country was occupied in 1944. The French government was more prepared to give up immigrant Jews than French Jews.

National-populism and race

As part of their campaign for respectability, contemporary fascists deny that they are racist. Following the New Right, they claim that the real racists are the architects of globalization and multiculturalism, who undermine national differences. The British National Party (BNP) maintains that it is not racist because

> 'Racism' is when you 'hate' another ethnic group. We don't 'hate' black people, we don't 'hate' Asians, we don't oppose any ethnic group for what God made them, they have a right to their own identity as much as we do, all we want to do is to preserve the ethnic and cultural identity of the British people. We want the same human rights as everyone else . . .
>
> www.bnp.org.uk/faq.html

Likewise David Duke, a former KKK member, set up the National Association for the Advancement of White People in order to make white nationalism more acceptable to the mainstream. It maintained that 'there should be equal rights and opportunities for all, including Whites'.

It is not difficult to expose the racist assumptions of national-populism. Take the BNP again. Firstly, it defines the nation in racist terms:

> the native peoples who have lived in these islands since before the Stone Age, and the relatively small numbers of peoples of almost identical stock, such as the Saxons, Vikings and Normans, and the Irish, who have come here and assimilated.

The biological foundations of BNP racism are confirmed by their opposition to mixed marriages, because 'all species and races of life on this planet are beautiful and must be preserved'. Ironically, given their drive for respectability, contemporary fascists owe much to the most exclusive biological racism.

Secondly, it's assumed that each race must be pure, and the duty of the state is to foster the 'uniqueness' of the people. National-populists advocate severe restrictions upon immigration and promote voluntary or forced repatriation. Preference in the job market would be given to 'natives', while commerce and industry would be restored to 'native' ownership. Perhaps it is expected, as the Nazis initially hoped, that ethnic minorities would find life so difficult that they would leave. The French FN certainly hopes that immigrants will be persuaded to leave the towns it governs.

Thirdly, national-populism frequently associates racism with a campaign to raise the birthrate of 'native' women. The BNP even appears to favour eugenicist spending on 'the healthy living in the first place [sic]' rather than on expensive operations for 'very old patients' suffering from a 'long-term complaint'.

Fourthly, for some national-populists the figure of the Muslim has taken over from that of the Jew as the embodiment of evil. Thus, in September 2001, following the destruction of the World Trade Center in New York by terrorist suicide pilots, mainstream Western politicians (with the exception of Berlusconi) carefully distinguished between majority Muslim opinion and a minority of zealots. Yet the BNP asserted that while not all Muslims were dangerous fanatics (liberal language again), Islam itself *was* dangerous. Just as Hitler believed the Jews were engaged in a campaign to 'Jewify' Germany, so the BNP believed that through 'indoctrination' in schools (that is, multi-faith religious education), high birth rates, and immigration, fundamentalists seek to turn Britain into an Islamic republic. As in inter-war Germany, anti-Islamic feeling is increasingly detached from the actual presence of Muslims, as the electoral advance of the xenophobic Danish People's Party confirms. Not all neo-fascists share this hatred of Islam. Many German neo-Nazis welcomed the 11 September attack by Islamic fundamentalists on their common enemy – America.

National-populism claims to be 'anti-racist' on the grounds that it favours equal rights for all races. Yet it demands the application of racial principles to immigration and social policy, and favours the departure of those considered racially undesirable. There are variations, however. The BNP calls for voluntary repatriation (although Griffin admits that he would prefer all non-whites to leave). The French FN prefers compulsion. Haider claims to have 'nothing against those who've been here for 20–30 years and made a living', only that he wants to turn away new arrivals.

It is uncertain how such policies would work out in practice. One major area of uncertainty is how those 'immigrants' who choose not to leave will be treated. Will they be treated equally in the job market and in the welfare system? One could expect conflicts between hard-liners and 'moderates' within national populist parties. It is certain that life would not be easy under national-populist rule for those considered ethnically alien.

The lesson of history is perhaps that the goal of racial homogenization is difficult to realize in practice, requires enormous compulsion and a radical break with democratic values. Even the Nazi regime's actions had contradictory results. To exterminate the

Jews, the Nazis had to mobilize enormous resources and negate everything hitherto considered decent. Even then, they failed to make Germany racially homogeneous. The war machine's desire for labour dictated the importation of seven million foreign workers and slaves by 1944. Although these labourers were subject to unimaginably harsh treatment, the regime could not prevent loving relations between Germans and foreigners. Paranoia about the effects of racial mixing simply drove the regime to greater, but equally futile, excess.

History also shows that the oppressiveness of racism is exacerbated by its arbitrariness. No-one has yet shown that tiny genetic differences between people living on opposite sides of boundaries or between people of different skin or hair colour are related to 'deep psychology', let alone daily behaviour. Neither has it been shown that cultural differences between peoples are greater than the differences among them. The vagueness of their principles permits racists to adapt their racism to whatever purpose they espouse. Earlier in the century it was customary to evoke the fundamentally different characteristics of Aryans and Latins. Now all Europeans are said to be united in a struggle against Islam. Some see the English and Irish as basically different, others do not. Needless to say, such disagreements are not the product of scientific investigation and advance. Racism remains a prejudice erected into a system.

In their *The Racial State*, Michael Burleigh and Wolfgang Wippermann argue that the Third Reich's subordination of all policy to the creation of a hierarchical racial new order made it a singular regime. Without wishing to deny the uniqueness of the Nazi regime – all regimes are both unique and susceptible to comparative analysis – I would wish to suggest that the prioritization of ultranationalism, usually with a strong racist element within it, is actually common to all fascist movements and regimes.

Chapter 9
Fascism and gender

Although fascists mentally prioritized racist nationalism, they conceived the nation in masculine terms. Indeed, fascism is a quintessentially male ideology, evoking the be-shirted street-fighter of the inter-war years and the skinhead of modern times. Fascism is as deeply opposed to feminism as it is to socialism. Historic fascists generally argued that women's primary function was domestic and reproductive. National-populists qualify this by saying that the sexes – like races – are 'equal but different'.

Many Europeans were convinced that the Great War had upset normal relations between the sexes. Women had taken male jobs, and were suspected of living independent and frivolous lives whilst men endured the nightmare of the front. The massive involvement of women in the war effort, meanwhile, stimulated the development of women's organizations, some of them feminist, and after the war women gained the vote in many countries. Bourgeois women adopted simpler forms of dress, more suited to working life, a fashion seen by some as de-sexing women. The French veteran, novelist, and future fascist Pierre Drieu La Rochelle lamented, 'this civilization no longer has sexes'.

The alleged crisis in gender relations was seen as a sign of general social decay. Radical workers or turbulent national minorities were thought to be affected by 'feminine' passions. Many conservatives felt that unless women were restored to their proper place, society could not function properly. These fears came together in the campaign, common to most European countries, to compensate for war deaths by raising the birth rate. These 'natalist' campaigns implied that women were primarily mothers, and should perhaps be forbidden other roles.

Fascists agreed that society must be regenerated by male values. Characteristically, they were more extreme and radical than conventional conservatives – indeed they dismissed conservatives as unmanly. Fascists saw war veterans as the repository of the virile national idea and the agents of the nation's regeneration. Service in the trenches proved an individual's devotion to the nation, and promoted masculine bravery, heroism, self-sacrifice, comradeship, the ability to endure suffering, and obedience – qualities that should be transferred to society as a whole. Codreanu called for 'a new type of hero in the warring sense, a social hero, a hero of work'. His model was the medieval king Stephen the Great, celebrated for his military prowess and fathering of children. These ideals were taken furthest in the SS, which represented a male martial order inspired by the Japanese Samurai, Teutonic Knights, and Jesuits.

Fascists did not value masculinity *per se* – only that of some male members of the dominant race. Socialists and communists (despite their own macho inclinations) were seen as the fomenters of 'feminine' indiscipline – while the fascist revolution was characterized by manly order. The Nazis saw the Jews and Poles as 'feminine' races, achieving their goals through devious plots rather than masculine openness.

It is no shock to discover that most fascists hated homosexuals. Some observers have considered that this homophobia resulted from the repressed homosexuality of fascists themselves: they point, for instance, to the homoerotic dress and lifestyle of the SS. One contemporary German neo-Nazi argues that homosexuality strengthens the bonds between true men. One might invoke the case of Ernst Röhm, leader of the Nazi SA. In many ways, he was typical of fascists, his facial scars a visible reminder of his war service and courage. He expected women to remain silent, and saw the Weimar Republic as an unmanly state characterized by female chattering, in which feminine Jews and Communists were too influential. In fact, the SA leader's homosexuality was widely known. He fended off accusations of unmanliness by espousing an intensely masculine activism.

There is no reason to believe that homosexuals are more numerous amongst fascists than in the rest of the population. The truth is probably more prosaic. Fascists were particularly hostile to homosexuals because they *feared* that their all-male communities would expose them to accusations of homosexuality. Furthermore, fascists believed that sexuality must be harnessed to reproduction of the race, which naturally implied heterosexuality.

Nevertheless, the fact that Röhm, a known homosexual, rose to the top of the Nazi hierarchy highlights the ability of fascism's populist, antibourgeois ethos to attract radicals of all shades, so long as they put the nation first. Röhm was not really a social or political radical. Rather he was a critic of 'bourgeois morality', who hoped that Nazism would have done with bourgeois hypocrisy and usher in a new manly order. Of course, those who interpreted the Nazi revolution in this way were a tiny minority, and they stood little chance of turning their dreams into reality. Röhm's 'perversion' was one of the pretexts for the suppression of the SA in June 1934. Thereafter the Nazis increased their persecution of homosexuals. No one knows how many died in concentration camps, or were 'treated' by Nazi doctors.

Many fascists were as contemptuous of women as they were of homosexuals, or at least they believed that women should remain in their 'proper place'. The Italian Futurist Filippo Marinetti was famous for his 'scorn for women'. Some Nazis campaigned against women's right to wear make-up or smoke in public. The Romanian

Iron Guard newspaper declared in 1937 that 'today's "intellectual" woman is an element utterly sterile for society'. Fascist regimes invariably implemented repressive measures against women. They attempted to remove women from the labour market and restrict their access to education. Whether in Germany, Italy, or Croatia, they expected women to produce the future citizens, soldiers, and mothers of the race. Women were to inculcate national values in their children, while the fascist drive for economic self-sufficiency made women important as consumers.

There was, however, a contradiction in these policies, for fascists wanted women in the home yet politicized functions once regarded simply as 'domestic': reproduction, education, and consumption all became national duties. Furthermore, in order to teach women their domestic duties, fascists mobilized them in organizations linked to the party – to return women to the home, fascism took them out of the home! At a time when conservative organizations (with the exception of some Catholic and peasant parties) rejected female membership, most fascist organizations possessed significant women's sections. In Italy there were some 2,000 female Fascists in 1921. Women's membership stagnated in the later 1920s, but rocketed during the regime's period of 'going to the masses' in the 1930s. At the time of the seizure of power, about 8% of the Nazi Party's membership were women. In 1931 women's sections were amalgamated into the National Socialist Frauenschaft (NSF) which, after the seizure of power, took control of all remaining women's groups. By 1938 the NSF had a paper membership of over two million. There may have been 100,000 or more women in French fascist organizations at their peak. More examples could be given.

In its mobilization of women, fascism differed significantly from authoritarian conservatism. The latter was antifeminist, and often established its own women's movements, but usually left room for women's groups to operate independently of the state (within 'civil society'). Fascists, in contrast, were deeply antipathetic to any

9. Female members of the British Union of Fascists salute Sir Oswald Mosley.

autonomous women's movement because they were afraid that it would put the interests of women above the nation. Nevertheless, fascists held that women could be incorporated into the nation only if their special needs and interests were recognized. So they made women's organizations part of the party or regime – just as they took over and attempted to incorporate the labour movement. Civil society was absorbed into fascism.

Surprisingly, most fascist parties attracted a few feminists. Mary Allen claimed that the British Union of Fascists represented the continuation of the pre-war Suffragette struggle. In Romania one could point to Alexandrina Cantacuzino, president of the Orthodox National Society of Romanian Women. In Italy Teresa Labriola, daughter of a famous syndicalist activist, believed that the Italian nation would be regenerated by a self-sacrificing female elite. In 1926 the Nazi Emma Hadlich argued that before foreign values had corrupted it, the Germanic race had been characterized by equality between the sexes. After the Nazi regime was established similar ideas were defended in a periodical, *The Nazi Fighter*.

Some misguided former feminists expected fascists to introduce female suffrage. In Italy the original fascist programme had included the right of women to vote. In countries where women already had the vote, such as Britain, some feminists were disappointed that female suffrage had not allowed them to win real political influence, and they hoped that fascism might remedy this. Many Italian women's organizations saw the liberal regime as unresponsive to women's concerns, and so favoured the nationalist opposition. During the Fascist years they championed 'Latin feminism' – a feminism said to be free of socialism and liberalism, which subordinated individual rights to tradition, family, and race.

Other feminists – often known as familial feminists – were less interested in political rights than in protecting women as women – they demanded measures against male alcoholism, reform of divorce laws, and improvement in women's rights as both mothers and workers. So long as such feminists were prepared to give up on representative democracy (a big if), they potentially had something in common with fascists, for they too stressed the role of the family in the national community.

Fascists also attracted the support of women engaged in apolitical or right-wing *anti*feminist movements. These women agreed with fascist men that women's place was in the home. For many bourgeois women, after all, the family offered certain privileges – control over children and domestic servants within an extended household. As 'carers' women could become involved in important charitable organizations, sometimes with influence on government policy. Such women attacked feminism – along with socialism, liberalism, and democracy – for undermining charity, the family, and the supply of domestic servants. Despite their deeply held conservatism, such women didn't always feel that conventional conservative organizations paid sufficient attention to the family. Poor rural women also voted for fascists in Germany, partly, perhaps, because they saw feminism as a fashion accessory adopted by bourgeois women.

Fascism, then, won support from a range of women's groups, feminist and non-feminist, formerly liberal, conservative, or even socialist. What they had in common was antipathy to the left, coupled with the conviction that existing parties, whether of left or right, didn't represent them properly. The engagement of women in fascist movements and regimes throws more light on the simultaneously radical and reactionary nature of fascism.

The most radical of the women who joined fascist movements and regimes did not fare well, for male activists (who had much more influence) had become fascists precisely out of a desire to restore the 'normal' relationship between the sexes. Mussolini soon lost interest in female suffrage and ensured that women's sections of the movement were subordinated to male branches. In Germany the aforementioned Emma Hadlich's views were refuted by Alfred

Rosenberg, who asserted that ancient German society had been patriarchal. In 1934 Hitler told Nazi women that there was no room for a battle of the sexes within Nazism. Both regimes became more concerned with persuading women to have children – the leader of the NSF, Gertrud Scholtz-Klink, led from the front by bearing eleven – and tried to restrict women's access to education and remove them from the labour market. The great majority of women within fascist movements were confined to activities generally considered to be suited to their nature – essentially welfare work.

This did not mean that women played a passive role in fascism. Even those engaged in apparently humble tasks such as knitting socks or collecting food for the poor were engaged in activity outside the home, as part of a complex organization directed largely by women (see Figure 10). Further up the hierarchy, the women's sections of fascist movements and regimes employed small armies of health visitors, nurses, domestic science teachers, and social workers. Male fascists might have seen women's work as secondary, but the women concerned did not. They struggled with men to extend their areas of competence, and attempted to invest their professions with a status equal to that of doctors and lawyers. For them, welfare was fundamental to the achievement of a harmonious, mobilized nation. While wishing to confine women to their 'sphere', male fascists agreed that women's work was essential to the realization of the mobilized nation. Women therefore had some leverage within fascist movements and regimes.

This influence came at great cost. Fascist movements demanded, and regimes implemented, a range of welfare provisions, many of which seemed to fulfil long-standing desires of the women's movement (family allowances, marriage loans, improved health care at work, and so on). These measures weren't meant to extend the range of choices open to women. They served, as we saw in Chapter 8, the supposed needs of the nation and race. In Germany, only Aryan women were considered sufficiently 'evolved' to be capable of fulfilling the maternal role or of bearing 'fit' children.

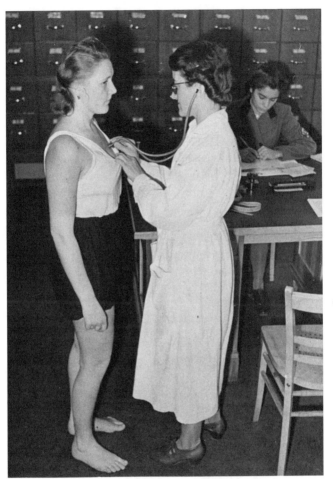

10. A female world. A doctor examines a new recruit to the Reich Community Service Agency, 6 September 1940.

Encouraged by Himmler, the SS went as far as to protect unmarried mothers – so long as they were racially acceptable. In France, the enormous welfare organizations of the Croix de feu and Parti social français refused aid to immigrants or their families.

In Italy mixing of races was regarded, before 1938 at least, as beneficial, and 'negative' eugenics were never endorsed. Yet the good of the race remained the goal of natalist policies. Italian policies were more authoritarian than those introduced in democratic states – 'impeding the fertility of the Italian people' through the promotion of birth control was designated a crime of state. Most significantly, welfare was distributed according to unofficial political criteria, so that those unfriendly to the regime didn't benefit. Although there are major differences between fascist regimes regarding the treatment of women, in all cases policy was harnessed to the creation of a permanently mobilized, homogeneous nation, whether defined biologically or not.

The position of women in contemporary national-populism is not dissimilar. The leader of the French National Front, Jean-Marie Le Pen, allotted to women the 'quasi-divine' mission of transmitting life and 'educating the hearts, minds, and sensibilities of children and adolescents'. The BNP proposes financial incentives for women to have children in order to combat the supposedly dangerous low birth rate and end discrimination against the family. Haider promised in the 1999 general election to distribute generous 'children's cheques' to mothers. As in the past, pro-natalism and racism are connected: since labour shortages will no longer be made up through immigration, women must have more babies, and it's implicit that only 'native' women will be encouraged to reproduce. Contemporary national-populism is heavily masculine in style, whether in Le Pen's belief that French chivalry is the answer to feminism, or in skinheads' football violence.

These policies issue from the fear, familiar to any student of the inter-war years, that women are taking over jobs for which they are not suited. As Le Pen says, interference in the normal allocation of tasks between the genders could lead 'men to take themselves for women, and women to take themselves for men'. In contemporary society, these fears are amplified by the chronic unemployment amongst a declining unskilled male working class, and by the conviction of some men that 'positive discrimination' in favour of women harms male promotion prospects. Furthermore, as the right becomes less worried about the danger from socialism and communism, issues related to gender roles, such as marriage, divorce, abortion, and sexuality have become more central to politics.

Women, nevertheless, join and vote for national-populists. Their position is somewhat different to that occupied by women in earlier fascist movements, for women's political and social position has improved, even if equality remains a long way off. Thanks to television, cinema, the decline of religious practice, and the changing nature of education, the range of options open to women is greater and their *expectations* are higher. Although most women reject the feminist label, they take for granted many of the conquests of feminism. This applies as much to bourgeois women who are elected on neo-fascist tickets as to the young working-class women who vote for national-populists. Le Pen, at least, has faced major difficulties in controlling the female members of his own family, some of whom occupy important positions within the movement. His ex-wife satirized his views on the family by appearing as a maid in a pornographic *Playboy* photo-shoot, while one of his daughters has broken with him over political tactics.

Fascist movements sometimes, as they did in the inter-war years, promise to respect the advances made by women. But they also advocate policies that would remove most of these gains. We cannot say how such tensions would work out in practice, but we can say that implementation of the extreme right's policies towards women would represent another radical break with liberal democracy.

Chapter 10
Fascism and class

At one time fascism was interpreted almost entirely in terms of its relationship to class. For Marxists, fascism was a dictatorship of the most reactionary elements of capitalism, or the expression of an alliance of dominant capitalists with a subordinate petty bourgeoisie. For Weberians, fascism represented a last-ditch bid by the 'traditional elites' to defend themselves against 'modernization'. We might at this stage add a further theory, also rooted in Weber, that sees fascism as a movement which 'essentially' expresses the petty bourgeoisie's equal hostility to big capital and organized labour.

Although Marxists and Weberians differ in the class they hold responsible for fascism (and in the way they define class), both seek to uncover in the actions, words, and writings of fascists and their allies evidence of the 'underlying interests' of the classes they see as crucial. Thus Marxists would regard the fascist prioritization of the national interest as a means for capitalists to combat socialist attempts to convince workers that class interests should be primary. Similarly, Weberians might read antisemitic texts as attempts to demonize the modern world in the person of the Jew or for evidence of the dilemmas of the petty bourgeoisie.

Totalitarian theorists, in contrast, argue that we must begin by understanding fascists' particular way of seeing the world. Fascists themselves claimed that ultranationalism was their motive force, and that the realization of the mobilized national community was their goal. So our task is to ask how far fascists achieved their objectives, and overcame the obstacles they confronted and the compromises they were forced to make. Class interest barely figures in the totalitarian approach.

Rather than revisit the strengths and weaknesses of the competing approaches, let us summarize the point of view I've advanced in the previous chapters.

1. In their own minds fascists made the realization of national unity, *as they defined it*, their central purpose. The fascist idea of the nation pervaded all aspects of policy.
2. The qualification 'as they defined it' is crucial: for fascists the nation was not an abstract idea, plucked out of thin air, but was constructed from all kinds of preconceptions, including predilections for the patriarchal family and existing property relations.
3. However, fascists defended the patriarchal family and employers' rights only insofar as they seemed compatible with those of the nation. 'Foreign' families or businesses would not enjoy protection. Unlike conservatives, fascists were not, therefore, absolute defenders of family or property.
4. As ultranationalists, fascists were necessarily opposed to all other 'isms'. Feminists and socialists were accused of putting gender, class, or humanity above the nation. Yet since fascists wanted to incorporate both genders and all classes into the nation, they were potentially willing to accept specific reforms advocated by feminists and socialists – *so long as these reforms were subordinated to the national interest as fascists defined it.*

Before we examine the practical implications of this for the relationship of fascism to class, it must be noted that there is nothing in fascism that *intrinsically* makes it appeal to any particular social class. Business might be attracted to a movement that seeks to destroy the labour movement in the name of national unity, yet employers might distrust a movement that is prepared to concede some socialist demands, and that places nation above property. Similarly, workers might oppose fascism because of its antisocialism, yet be attracted by its promise to put the interests of native workers ahead of those of foreigners.

Only through an examination of fascism *in context* can we explain who actually supported fascism and why. We have to look at the situation from two angles. Firstly, we have to examine the social make-up and motivations of fascist supporters. Secondly, we have to analyse the way in which the strategies and attitudes of fascist activists themselves shaped the appeal of fascism.

Activists and voters

There is much variation in support for fascism in class terms. Most historians agree that farmers and the petty bourgeoisie (especially artisans, civil servants, retail employees, and supervisory personnel) were over-represented in the much-studied Nazi electorate, but that the Nazis also gained considerable support from workers and the upper class. The Nazi Party was stronger in certain classes, but it was more of an 'all-class' party than were any of its rivals.

French fascism in the inter-war years shows a similarly broad appeal combined with over-representation of the middle classes. When we look more closely we find some intriguing differences. Whereas in Germany private-sector white-collar workers and teachers preferred the Nazis, their counterparts in France were attracted to the left. If we move to Hungary, we find stronger working-class and landless labourer support for fascism. Romanian fascism was mainly backed by peasants and students. National-populism differs again. Most is known about the French National Front, which recruits voters pretty equally from all classes.

If we take into account other influences on the fascist vote, the picture becomes still more complex. In Germany we find that Protestant workers in smaller industries were likely to vote Nazi, while Catholic workers voted for the Catholic Centre or the Communists, and Protestant workers in large industries voted for the socialists. In France, we discover that the Catholic bourgeoisie in industrialized and urban France were more likely to join fascist organizations than were the Catholic bourgeoisie of rural areas or the anticlerical bourgeoisie of the towns. We also find that male workers in French heavy industry were less likely to join fascist trade unions than were female workers in the textile industry.

Further examples would add only confusion. The point is that along with class, gender, geography, and religion influenced votes for fascists. Fascism has no special appeal to any social class – the variations described above actually tell us as much about political circumstances in individual countries as they do about fascism. We might add that the diversity of political attitudes in any given class suggests that its members must have disagreed on where their interests lay.

This points to the second aspect of the question of fascism and class – the role of activists. Too often, activists are seen as representatives of 'underlying' social forces – thus socialist activists are said to 'speak for' the working class, and conservative or fascist activists are said (even if they don't know it) to 'speak for' the bourgeoisie. Anyone who knows political activists will realize that they aren't quite like the rest of us. They feel that they possess privileged insight into the organization of the world and have a mission to persuade the rest of us of the validity of their views. The socialist activist, for example, doesn't just articulate the workers' feelings – she or he tries to *persuade* the worker that her or his interest lies in embracing their brand of socialism, not a rival socialist school, political Catholicism, or even fascism. So activists don't just reflect the views of those they seek to represent – they play a considerable part in shaping the way in which people conceive their 'interests'. We must take seriously those who formulated party propaganda and decided to whom it should be directed.

Let us take Nazism as an illustration. Although Nazism was particularly popular amongst farmers and the petty bourgeoisie, its appeal was broader than that of its rivals (the socialists appealed especially to the male working class, communists to the male unemployed, and the Catholic Centre to the Catholic minority). Whereas these latter parties cast their programme in class or confessional terms, the Nazis appealed to voters as members of the nation. The Nazis set themselves up as representatives of 'the people' and claimed to express popular opposition to a corrupt and foreign political establishment – potentially a very broad appeal indeed. They were able to channel the resentment of small shopkeepers into attacks on 'Jewish' department store owners. They won the support of many workers by incorporating the symbols used by the left – such as red flags modified with swastikas, or the grinning, gluttonous, top-hatted, cigar-smoking capitalist – into a nationalist and antisemitic programme. They told workers that their enemy was not business, but Jewish business. This nationalist anticapitalism had the advantage of being relatively attractive to many employers, too, for it potentially spared German capitalists the blame for the workers' plight.

The Nazis were most successful in becoming what all fascists have attempted to be – national parties, amalgamating otherwise antagonistic groups into a single movement. We must not, however, regard the success of such a policy as automatic. Nationalism does not have an inherently broader appeal than class – it all depends how nation and class are defined. The Nazi conception of the nation was influenced by conscious and unconscious 'biases'. Many Nazis saw Germany as intrinsically Protestant or even pagan, a view which excluded Catholics from their electorate. In France, Italy, and Spain, in contrast, fascists defined the nation as Catholic, and so excluded anticlericals. In

Romania, Codreanu equated Romanian Orthodoxy with the nation, and so followers of the Uniate faith were excluded from the nation – and from the Legion.

The appeal of fascism in class terms is best understood as the product of an interaction between the strategies of fascist activists (with their unacknowledged biases) and the circumstances of particular groups (with their unacknowledged biases). The resulting variability doesn't mean that fascism's class composition is unimportant. On the contrary, it mattered very much, because those who placed their hopes in fascism differed greatly in the amount of power available to them. All classes weren't equally helpless beneath the rifle butt, as Marx might have said. I want to illustrate this through a brief examination of two key terms in the fascist lexicon: national socialism and corporatism.

National socialism

The term national socialism was not used by the Nazis alone. Back in 1898 Maurice Barrès presented the electoral programme of the 'National Socialist Republican Committee' of Nancy:

> Against a policy that aims only to satisfy animosities, and of which the only driving force is the lust for power, I come anew to oppose the *national* and *social* ideas which you have already acclaimed and which you will not today repudiate.
>
> [. . .] In the top ranks of society, in the heart of the provinces, in the moral and material sphere, in commerce, industry, agriculture, even in the shipyards where they compete with French workers, foreigners are poisoning us like parasites.
>
> One vital principle that should underlie the new French policy is to protect all its nationals against this invasion, and to be aware of that brand of socialism that is so cosmopolitan, or rather so German, that it would weaken the country's defences.

For Barrès, internationalist socialism – Marxism – constituted a menace to the French nation, indeed to the French race, for it was a 'German' ideology. He called for a socialism that would be national in two senses: it would protect only those workers with roots in the national soil and it would reconcile hitherto opposed classes by ensuring that each subordinated its special interests to the national good.

Barrès called not for the suppression of property but for a change in the *spirit* of class relations. This formula was less scary for capitalists than was Marxism. Yet Barrès proposed reforms such as a graduated income tax and profit sharing, which might seem tame to contemporary eyes, but which were opposed absolutely – even hysterically – by mainstream conservative opinion at the time. Neither were local steel magnates enthralled by Barrès's desire to stem the flow of cheap foreign labour. In the event, Barrès's programme did appeal to some disenchanted conservatives in Nancy, but not to enough to get him elected.

Twenty-seven years later, Hitler, to whom the judge had granted a degree of latitude unusual for a defendant, addressed the jurors at his trial for his part on the Beer-Hall putsch:

> The National Socialist movement of what was then the Workers' Party adopted as its first principle the realisation that the Marxist movement was to be fought to the end; second the realisation that the revolution [of 1918], as the consequence of Marxism and of an unprecedented criminal act was not a matter of the German bourgeoisie becoming national once more: the problem is that the German working people, the broad masses, must be made national again. That means not just a pure, I mean passive, relationship to nationalism, but an active fight against those who have ruined it until now. Besides, it is ridiculous to want to nationalise a people at a time when hundreds of thousands are working on all sides to de-nationalise the people, and these hundreds of thousands, who also brought about the revolution, do

not even belong to the race. Thus the Marxist problem has become a racial problem, the most serious and deepest problem of the day.

Hitler might not have shared Barrès's literary gifts, but his assumptions were similar. Internationalist Marxist socialism is the enemy of the German race, and to fight it the workers must be reincorporated into the nation. *National* socialism reconciles the classes.

Corporatism

Like fascists everywhere, Hitler saw corporatism, sometimes dismissed by contemporary scholars as a smokescreen for the untrammelled power of big business, as one of the keys to social peace. Corporatism is not, however, intrinsically fascist. At its simplest it means that decisions about policy are taken by organized bodies representing the interests concerned – trade unions, employers' organizations, groups representing families or farmers, and so on – rather than by the government or parliament. At one time or another, most post-war Western democracies have practised corporatism, in that trade unions and employers' groups have had a say in the elaboration of policy.

Fascist corporatism differs in that it is predicated upon destruction or purging of existing associations, for it was assumed that once unpatriotic left-wing or 'foreign' influences had been eliminated, the natural patriotism of all classes would re-emerge. Another premise was that corporatism would protect workers from the exploitation to which they were subject in a free market – in which wages were at the mercy of the capitalist's whim. Class conflict would give way to harmony within the nation.

It remained to be settled what concessions capitalists would be expected to make in order to entice workers back into the national community. Especially important was the amount of autonomy to

11. A Spanish worker salutes a parade of the Falange in 1937. The Falange prided themselves on the originality of their programme for the workers.

be accorded to fascist unions in the corporatist system. In many countries those who wanted the greatest degree of freedom for workers' unions were known as 'syndicalists'.

In Italy, the heirs of the INA disagreed with radical Fascists on the nature of corporatism. Broadly speaking, the former emphasized state control over corporatist bodies. Meanwhile, technocrats around Bottai wanted more power for managers and engineers. The most radical – syndicalists and Fascist trade unionists – wanted more autonomy for workers' unions. Business generally opposed any form of compulsory corporatism as a constraint upon free enterprise – whilst asking the state to provide legal backing for their own price-fixing cartels!

In 1925 Fascist unions launched strikes in the metal-working industry in a bid to impose their syndicalist views. Under the Palazzo Vidoni agreement of October 1925 they obtained a monopoly of workers' representation – to the annoyance of business, which saw Fascist unions as nearly as dangerous as socialist bodies. Yet the unions failed to obtain parity with employers' organizations in the corporatist structure which began to be put in place at the same time. Business interests won out because strikes were banned and unions were declared to be agents of the state. Business still feared Bottai's endeavour to ensure that decisive power was in the hands of managers and engineers, rather than big business, yet it cannot be denied that the partisans of fascist trade unionism failed to achieve their ends.

The Nazi Party also included a strong trade union wing in the form of its factory cell organization, the NSBO. After 1933 NSBO leaders, thinking their day had dawned, threatened bosses with concentration camps if they didn't pay higher wages. Hitler's suppression of the SA in 1934, partly as a result of conservative pressure, was a heavy blow to radicals. Already in 1933 the NSBO had been incorporated within the corporatist German Labour Front (DAF). In practice the destruction of left-wing unions and the banning of strikes, together with endorsement of management's right to manage, ensured that German workers lacked collective representation. Yet like other Nazi agencies, the Labour Front did provide jobs and advancement for ideologically committed workers, and it became one of the 'fiefdoms' which undermined the old state hierarchy. The Nazis also retained much of Weimar's welfare system and set up a 'Strength Through Joy' movement to regulate workers' leisure – but harnessed these to their racial and eugenic projects. Welfare served the goal of incorporating all classes into an ethnically pure, militarily strong national community.

The fortunes of peasants and artisans in the two fascist regimes were similar to those of workers. Both Fascists and Nazis had promised to restore the position and prestige of these classes, yet achieved little in practice. The Italian regime's promises of land to the smallholding peasantry were largely unfulfilled. Mussolini's campaign to prevent rural depopulation didn't prevent the population of Rome from doubling during the life of the regime. In Germany, Nazi shopkeeper and artisan organizations were given little freedom of action. Promises to suppress department stores were broken, while big business rather than small benefited from the confiscation of Jewish property. The Nazis kept their promises to help indebted peasants, yet it turned out that this was insufficient to prevent the decline of the rural population.

Radical fascism was more than a device to fool the lower classes, for many fascists were prepared to go to great lengths to realize its goals. Radical fascism failed not because it was not meaningful, but because it lacked the power to achieve its ends. The national interest was never strong enough to 'discipline' savage capitalism, especially as capitalists and many fascists believed a strong capitalism to be in the national interest. Anyway, both regimes saw big business as essential to war production, and gave such firms priority in the allocation of raw materials and labour.

The position of the workers was not, however, defined simply by their subservience to capitalism (any more than the position of the bourgeois women who staffed fascist welfare organizations was defined just by subservience to men). Recent research into 'everyday life' under Nazism suggests that whilst older workers in particular remained hostile to Nazism, many redirected aspirations for a better-organized society, previously expressed by socialist parties, into Nazism. The Social Democrats, after all, had never been immune to nationalist feeling. Once socialism had proved its ineffectiveness in 1932–3, the Nazis seem to have had some success in winning over formerly socialist workers. It has even been suggested that working-class soldiers regarded participation in the regime's race crimes in the east as an extension of the 'high-quality German work' they had once turned out in the factories. In effect, in return for abandoning class solidarities, workers were offered minor parts in a national elite and a share of the benefits of foreign conquest. In Germany, in defiance of the values of the international labour movement, workers lorded it over millions of slave labourers. In Italy, too, the division of labour was quasi-racial, with northern workers occupying skilled jobs and southerners in the less enviable positions.

Business and fascism

Does all this mean that fascism was 'ultimately' a business ideology, as some Marxists have suggested? Yes, in the sense that some business interests in both Germany and Italy joined fascist movements, and once in power big business supported fascism, and viewed the destruction of the labour movement positively.

No, in the sense that whilst capitalists in many countries were happy to use fascist bands to fight the left, relatively few capitalists actually wanted to install fascist regimes. In Italy, right up to the Fascist seizure of power, business remained divided in political allegiance between the INA and Giolitti's liberalism. In Germany, big business did much to undermine democracy, yet the majority of business people would have preferred a conservative dictatorship, with Nazi support, to a Hitler government. Agrarian interests were more active than big business in the negotiations that finally brought Hitler to power.

No, again, in the sense that to describe fascism as a capitalist regime is not saying much, for big business has shown an enormous ability to adapt to regimes to which it is opposed in principle. Neither is it likely that only recourse to fascism could have saved German or Italian capitalism in the inter-war period. Some businessmen joined fascist movements in the belief that this was so, but there's little reason to believe that they were right. It's not inconceivable that business more generally *might* have seen fascism as the only possible way of ensuring the survival of capitalism. Yet it happens that in the particular historical circumstances of Italy in 1922 and Germany in 1933 most business people didn't see things this way.

12. **Nazism and private property: the Aryanization of a Jewish owned shop in Frankfurt am Main c.1938. The sign reads Stamm & Bassermann formerly Gummi Weil.**

This reminds us that fascism did not defend property absolutely, any more than it did the family. Fascist regimes regulated business in the national interest especially for the pursuit of war, whilst destroying business's capability of intervening as a body in political decision-making. The Italian regime built up a strong nationalized sector in the 1930s. True, private industry continued to prosper, but the strength of the public sector helped to alienate conservatives from the regime during the war. Most strikingly, the Nazi regime expropriated Jewish property. In Eastern Europe, fascists threatened to expropriate huge sections of business, on the grounds that it was ethnically alien, and they were bitterly opposed by conservatives for this reason.

Marxists might object that many people, including business people, joined fascist movements out of hostility to Marxism, and that fascist ultranationalism represented a deliberate attempt to undermine workers' class loyalties. This is all true. Yet it's quite another thing to argue that fascism was *ultimately* a means of defending capitalism. The ultranationalist ideas on which fascists drew contained a plethora of other motivations, conceptions, and ideas, from which the question of capitalism was never absent, yet where it was never dominant either.

Chapter 11
Fascism and us

Fascism and modernization

In Chapter 7 we saw that fascism bequeathed a legacy of hitherto
marginal replica movements and a number of more successful
national-populist groups. In this section I want to explore the
inheritance of fascism through discussion of an ongoing debate
about whether fascism represented, perhaps inadvertently, a force
which helped to bring into being the 'modern' world, or whether
it represented a failed attempt to restore 'traditional' society.
Partisans of the latter view could point to the support of so-called
antimodern classes – artisans, peasants, and aristocratic
landowners – for fascism. Some fascist policies can be seen as
antimodern – the return to the land, restriction of city growth, and
idealization of the peasantry. Codreanu's fondness for peasant
costume expressed Romanian fascism's desire for a return to
peasant sources and was typical of fascism. Other evidence suggests
that fascism was 'modern': the worship of military technology;
favouritism towards big business in the distribution of military
contracts in Italy and Germany; mass mobilization; the
involvement of women in fascist movements; the promotion of
commercialized sport; and so on.

Evidence can be piled on either side without resolving the question
(unless one claims that the evidence that doesn't fit is 'secondary').

The problem really lies with the concept of modernization itself, for at the end of two centuries of 'modernization', attitudes that might be seen as non-modern – racism, for example – seem as deeply rooted in Western societies as ever. It is in any case doubtful that history 'normally' moves towards liberal-democratic, secular, rationalist, industrial society, or that we can perceive the necessary direction of history at all. Lacking such insight, observers tend to judge fascism's modernity in terms of what they personally regard as 'progressive'. A scholar who regards social mobility for workers as desirable would see workers' access to administrative jobs under fascism as a sign of 'modernization'. Scholars (happily) regard racism negatively, so they interpret racism as 'antimodern'.

The German historians' quarrel (*Historikerstreit*) of the 1980s illustrated the danger of uncritical use of the modernization concept. The *Historikerstreit* was precipitated by Martin Broszat's call for historians to ask more sophisticated questions about Nazism, rather than simply condemn it morally. Unfortunately, this sensible suggestion was obscured by his conviction that this goal could be achieved by examining Nazism's role in promoting or restraining tendencies towards modernization in German society. Introduction of the term 'modernization' dragged assumptions about the 'normal' and desirable course of history into the debate. Thus Broszat's argument that the welfare policies of the Nazi Labour Front paved the way for the social policies of modern Germany permitted critics to accuse him of presenting Nazism in a positive light. With some justice he was said to have artificially isolated a long-term modernization process from other aspects of Nazism, and therefore to have neglected the intrinsically racist nature of Nazi welfare. Other historians argued that Robert Ley's German Labour Front intended to construct a more 'modern' society in which individual merit mattered more than group membership in determining an individual's social status, but they forgot that in Nazi Germany advancement was restricted by gender and race.

To be useful, the term 'modernization' must be precisely defined. Some ask simply whether fascism altered existing social structures – amongst other things they explore the position of women or workers. In this diluted sense, modernization becomes merely a euphemism for change. It generates worthwhile questions, but doesn't presume to tell us whether change was 'modern'.

Another possibility is to reformulate Broszat's question so that we ask whether fascism contributed to the emergence and characteristics of subsequent regimes, without making assumptions about 'normality'. Thus, we find that fascist welfare legislation in both Italy and Germany was partly incorporated into that of successor regimes. It's also possible that the role played by women in the administration of welfare prepared the way for greater female public engagement after the war, while Mosley's fascination with Keynesian economics might have anticipated post-war social democracy. Historians have also suggested that fascist leisure programmes helped to 'de-proletarianize' workers and prepare the way for post-war individualist consumer society. Such continuities are not, however, evidence of the operation of an inevitable tendency towards 'modernization' present in all regimes. They were unintended and unforeseen – even accidental – consequences of particular historical circumstances, liable to modification as conditions changed.

Furthermore, the question of continuity is complex. Fascist welfare policy was consciously shaped by ultranationalism, political discrimination, and racism. It therefore differed significantly from that of liberal democracies which generally espouse universal principles and endorse the rights of all individuals to equal treatment. Yet the discriminatory tendencies of fascist social policies persist beneath the surface of modern systems, and this might be seen as providing fertile ground for the explicit discrimination favoured by national-populists.

Given the difficulty of determining what is 'modern', another approach might be to examine how fascists *perceived* the question of modernization (and even whether they thought in these terms at all). Just as there were many views of what national or class interests meant, there were different views of modernity. Fascism was one of several possible ways of responding to the upheavals of the past two centuries.

Fascists espoused a worldview inspired partly by what at the time passed as modern and scientific. They drew upon Social Darwinism and its French alternative, Lamarckianism, collective psychology, social biology, the science of crowds, and studies of myths. Linking all of these were 'scientific' assumptions about national characters and/or races. This 'science' was married to the conviction that the nation must be internally strong and homogeneous, if it was to overcome the unavoidable tendency to decadence and survive in the life-and-death international struggle. Here fascists' ideas were shaped by artistic modernism, which perceived the world as a dark, threatening place in which nothing was permanent, which nonetheless might be made sense of and even tamed through the special techniques of the artist.

Fascists called for the harnessing of the ethnically acceptable elements of both genders and all classes to the national purpose, and to the struggle for economic self-sufficiency within a national sphere of influence or empire. Although the emphasis differed, most fascists believed that the nation must reconcile modern imperatives with national traditions, by balancing rural and urban needs, for instance. This was not science as we know it. Yet many fascists saw their project as a necessary response to the modern world. Others interpreted it as a necessary return to tradition, and still others as a reconciliation of tradition and modernity. Beyond this uncertainty we cannot go. Fascism is a contradictory set of interrelated and contested ideologies and practices which cannot easily be categorized in terms of straightforward binary opposites such as tradition and modernity.

Fascism and antifascism

Does the unprecedented intolerance, violence, and, in the Nazi case, exterminationist nature of fascism mean that more than any other subject it must be studied from a moral point of view? Do we have to write from an explicitly antifascist position? Must we write about fascism with the intention of preventing it from happening again?

The answers are not simple. We must begin by distinguishing between the academic study and moral judgement of fascism. Academics use the concept of fascism to try to make sense of the past and present, and to explain fascism's *whys* and *hows*. Thanks to their professional training, historians, sociologists, and political scientists can justifiably claim to have a special ability to answer these sorts of questions. Academics do not, however, have any monopoly on the question of what *should* have been or *ought* to be. Moral positions just cannot be deduced from the study of the past. Historians can depict the actions of fascism as gruesomely as they wish – alas, fascists' actions will be seen as *crimes* only if the reader shares the moral perspective of the writer. Academics are not the judges of morality.

Those who regard academics' refusal to moralize as dereliction of the scholar's duty will protest. Didn't professional academics use scholarly neutrality to claim that the rise of fascism could not concern them? Worse, didn't academics use their academic skills to justify fascist policies? All this is true, but I would wish to maintain that the approach to fascism outlined in this book does not represent an abdication of moral responsibility.

Firstly, morality is a question for *all* members of society. As citizens, academics have as much right, and as great a duty, as anyone to judge – so long as they remember that they do so as citizens. It would be arrogant of academics to claim to have any special insight into *ought* questions. At most, historians can point out the complexities of moral choices in the past, while sociologists and political scientists might play a part in the conception and evaluation of government policy – under democratic control.

Indeed, it was the very conviction of German and Italian academics that their 'scientific' methods provided them with special knowledge of the public good that permitted them to intervene in other people's lives without their consent. It was precisely the belief that medical science had resolved moral questions that permitted the involvement of doctors in the Holocaust. Likewise, fascists and their heirs confuse science and morality when they claim that since category A *have* lived in such and such a country for X number of centuries, category A alone *should* live there.

Secondly, the methods used by the professional academics who backed Nazism and Fascism were fundamentally different to those advocated here. Although one cannot afford to be complacent, contemporary academics endeavour, so far as they can, to take nothing for granted. They subject their own assumptions, and those of their colleagues, to systematic criticism, and they try, if not always successfully, to uncover unacknowledged prejudices in their work.

The Italian and German professional academics who collaborated with Fascism and Nazism, in contrast, started from the assumption that certain ways of seeing the world were beyond question. For instance, Italian historians agreed that history could be properly understood only in terms of the development of the nation-state, and that the nation had a fundamental character, the preservation of which *ought* to be the object of state policy. Likewise, German scholars founded their histories on the concept of the racialized *volk*. Hence their willingness to collaborate with Nazism.

In fact, the idea of national character is mere prejudice which crumbles away under the most limited scrutiny. The science of fascists is little more than bigotry erected into a system. A proper scholarly method is intrinsically antifascist, in that it treats sceptically what fascists regard as beyond criticism. To say this, however, is not enough to defend academic research against those who see it as a form of 'ivory tower' detachment, for it might legitimate a complacent pursuit of academic interests while the world collapses around them. One answer is that the questions we ask of the past are inspired partly by our moral purposes. So it's quite legitimate to study fascism in order to discover which means have been most effective in combating it and what might help fight fascism in the future. (Sadly, others might study fascism in order to resuscitate it.) Nevertheless, caution is required, for the study of fascism alone cannot provide antifascist strategies.

Firstly, as emphasized at the outset, using the concept of fascism provides only a partial insight into specific cases, for an individual movement will possess features explicable only in terms of its particular circumstances. Since no 'pure' example of fascism could ever exist, we need to deploy other concepts alongside that of fascism. The problem is not just that a fascist movement is 'adapted' to local conditions – this would imply that a movement has a primary fascist core plus secondary contextual features. It is actually impossible to determine the relative importance of local and general features, since both are essential to the character of the movement. To understand individual movements we need to deploy a range of concepts, and to acknowledge that there will be as many antifascisms as there are fascisms. If strategy was based entirely upon analysis of historic fascism, it would inevitably fail to take into account novel features of the far right today.

Secondly, the elaboration of an antifascist strategy requires analysis of antifascism as well as fascism. This subject is outside the scope of this book, but we can say that historical research reveals that no single method has been universally effective against fascism. Banning fascist organizations sometimes works, sometimes it doesn't. There's no telling whether prosecutions for racist propaganda will represent a deterrent or promote sympathy for the victims of 'injustice'. There are some cases in which the efforts of conservatives to appease racism in the electorate have deprived fascists of support, but other cases in which this has legitimated fascism. Clearly, potential supporters of fascism have to be offered a better and more humane alternative means of combating their problems. But there is no imperative that says that this alternative must be revolutionary (as some Marxists claim), or democratic.

Ultimately, the strategies chosen will depend as much on moral choices as to what is an acceptable means of fighting fascism as upon scholarly assessments of what has happened in the past. Is it morally acceptable, for instance, to combat fascism by appropriating its racism? Such questions are for society as a whole, not just for academics.

What are the prospects for fascism today? If there is one thing that we should learn from history, it is that prediction is a risky business. So far, however, no movement that openly assumes the mantle of historic fascism has come close to making a political breakthrough. The explanation for this failure is not only that for most people fascism evokes fear, but that many of the features of inter-war society that made fascism what it was – for example, the medical profession's belief in eugenics, the conviction that national security depended on a high birth rate among the 'native' population and economic autarky, and young men's predilection for uniforms and marching – are not so evident in contemporary society. Nevertheless, there are neo-Nazi movements in most Western countries. Fascism remains an 'available option', and there is no reason to suppose that fascists could not gain power in circumstances quite different to those pertaining in the inter-war years. Modern society, after all, depends on a potentially fragile network of trust and negotiation, which could easily come crashing down.

At the moment the prospects for national-populism are rather better than those of fascism proper, as the rise of the far right in France, Switzerland, Denmark, Austria, the United States, and

Russia demonstrates. The prevalence of racism in the West, the demonization of Islam, fears that globalization is corroding nation-states, the belief that immigrants will undermine some ill-defined national identity, and the conviction that politicians are all corrupt suggest that further victories might be on the way. It would be complacent to assume that democracy is now so deeply rooted as to make it impossible for the extreme right to win power, for democracy itself is not free from discriminatory tendencies. Democracy *is* deeply rooted, but it is not always connected to a belief that all human beings deserve equal treatment. For many, it means simply the right of the majority to do as it wishes, and national-populism has successfully exploited this conviction.

The success of Jean-Marie Le Pen in reaching the second round of the French presidential election of 2002 demonstrates the ingrained strength of national-populist racism in certain areas of Europe, while his crushing defeat on the second ballot reveals the extent of opposition to the extreme right in the rest of society. Both the profitability of the extreme right's 'electoral' strategy and its limits were exposed. Whether national-populists will ever be able to convince a broader section of the population that it really could solve all social and economic problems through the ending of immigration and the return of women to the home is open to question. Furthermore, while many people seem psychologically troubled by the notion that the benefits of democracy might be appropriated by people who are not 'like us', or who are considered 'undeserving' in some way, they might be less ready to give these advantages up themselves. Would women be happy to see themselves forced out of the job market? How would the inevitable labour shortages and loss of purchasing power caused by the departure of immigrants be dealt with? The inevitable problems might be 'resolved' peacefully. It is equally possible that a cycle of violence and counter-violence might be unleashed, and that authoritarianism, and even full-blown fascism, might emerge.

References

Hannah Arendt, *The Origins of Totalitarianism* (Harcourt, Brace & Co., 1951)

Bessel, Richard (ed.), *Fascist Italy and Nazi Germany: Comparisons and Contrasts* (Cambridge University Press, 1996)

Blinkhorn, Martin, *Fascists and Conservatives: The Radical Right and the Establishment in Twentieth-Century Europe* (Unwin Hyman, 1990)

Blinkhorn, Martin, *Fascism and the Right in Europe 1919–1945* (Longman, 2000)

Bosworth, R. J. B., *The Italian Dictatorship: Problems and Perspectives in the Interpretation of Mussolini and Fascism* (Arnold, 1998)

Burleigh, Michael and Wolfgang Wippermann, *The Racial State, Germany 1933–1945* (Cambridge University Press, 1993)

Burleigh, Michael, *The Third Reich: A New History* (Macmillan, 2001)

De Grand, Alexander, *Italian Fascism: Its Origins and Development* (University of Nebraska Press, 1982)

De Grazia, Victoria, *How Fascism Ruled Italian Women: Italy, 1922–1945* (University of California Press, 1992)

Dobratz, Betty E. and Stephanie L. Shanks-Meile, *'White Power, White Pride': The White Separatist Movement in the United States* (Johns Hopkins University Press, 2000)

Durham, Martin, *The Christian Right, the Far Right and the Boundaries of American Conservatism* (Manchester University Press, 2000)

Eatwell, Roger, *Fascism: A History* (Vintage, 1996)

Eatwell, Roger, 'Towards a New Model of Generic Fascism', *Journal of Theoretical Politics*, 4 (1992), pp. 161–194

Peter Fritzsche, 'Nazi Modern', *Modernism/Modernity*, 3(1) (1996), pp. 1–21

Griffin, Roger, *The Nature of Fascism* (Pinter, 1991)

Griffin, Roger, *Fascism* (Oxford University Press, 1995)

Griffin, Roger, *International Fascism: Theories, Causes and the New Consensus* (Arnold, 1998)

Laclau, Ernsto, 'Fascism and Ideology' and 'Toward a Theory of Populism' in *Politics and Ideology in Marxist Theory : Capitalism, Fascism, Populism* (NLB, 1977)

Ioanid, Radu, *The Sword of the Archangel : Fascist Ideology in Romania*, tr. Peter Heinegg (East European Monographs, 1990)

Kershaw, Ian and Moshe Lewin (eds.), *Stalinism and Nazism: Dictatorships in Comparison* (Cambridge University Press, 1996)

Kershaw, Ian, *Hitler*, 2 vols (Allen Lane, 1998–2000)

Koonz, Claudia, *Mothers in the Fatherland: Women, the Family, and Nazi Politics* (St Martin's Press, 1987)

Mosse, George L., *The Fascist Revolution: Towards a General Theory of Fascism* (Howard Fertig, 1999)

Passmore, Kevin (ed.), *Women, Gender and Fascism in Europe, 1919–1945* (Manchester University Press, 2002)

Payne, Stanley, *A History of Fascism 1919–1945* (University of Wisconsin Press, 1995)

Renton, Dave, *Fascism: Theory and Practice* (Pluto Press, 1999)

Simmons, Harvey G., *The French National Front: The Extremist Challenge to Democracy* (Westview, 1996)

Woolf, S. J., *Fascism in Europe* (Methuen, 1968)

Index

Expand your collection of
VERY SHORT INTRODUCTIONS

Visit the
VERY SHORT INTRODUCTIONS
Web site

www.oup.co.uk/vsi

➤ **Information** about all published titles

➤ News of **forthcoming books**

➤ **Extracts** from the books, including titles not yet published

➤ **Reviews** and views

➤ **Links** to other **web sites** and main OUP web page

➤ Information about **VSIs in translation**

➤ **Contact** the editors

➤ **Order** other **VSIs** on-line